BASIC for IBM® Personal Computers

Little, Brown Microcomputer Bookshelf Series

Banse, Timothy
Home Applications and Games for the VIC 20

Banse, Timothy
Home Applications and Games for the Apple II and IIe

Banse, Timothy
Home Applications and Games for the Atari 400/800™ and 1200XL™

Barnett, Michael P. and Graham K. Barnett
Personal Graphics for Profit and Pleasure on the APPLE® II Plus Computer

Morrill, Harriet
BASIC for IBM® Personal Computers

Morrill, Harriet
Mini and Micro BASIC: Introducing Applesoft®, Microsoft®, and BASIC Plus

Nahigian, J. Victor and William S. Hodges
Computer Games for Businesses, Schools, and Homes

Nahigian, J. Victor and William S. Hodges
Computer Games for Business, Schools, and Homes for TRS-80 Level II BASIC

Orwig, Gary W. and William S. Hodges
The Computer Tutor: Learning Activities for Homes and Schools (for the TRS-80®, Apple®, and PET/CBM® Home Computers)

Orwig, Gary W. and William S. Hodges
The Computer Tutor: ATARI® Home Computer Edition (for the ATARI® 400/ 800™, 600XL™, 800XL™, 1200XL™, 1400XL™, and 1450 XLD™ Home Computers and the ATARI® VCS 2600™/5200™ Computer Keyboards)

Windeknecht, Thomas G.
6502 Systems Programming

Little, Brown Computer Systems Series

Basso, David T., and Ronald D. Schwartz
Programming with FORTRAN/WATFOR/ WATFIV

Chattergy, Rahul, and Udo W. Pooch
Top-down, Modular Programming in FORTRAN with WATFIV

Coats, R. B., and A. Parkin
Computer Models in the Social Sciences

Conway, Richard, and David Gries
An Introduction to Programming: A Structured Approach Using PL/I and PL/C, Third Edition

Conway, Richard, and David Gries
Primer on Structured Programming: Using PL/I, PL/C, and PL/CT

Conway, Richard, David Gries, and E. Carl Zimmerman
A Primer on Pascal, Second Edition

Cripps, Martin
An Introduction to Computer Hardware

Easley, Grady M.
Primer for Small Systems Management

Finkenaur, Robert G.
COBOL for Students: A Programming Primer

Freedman, Daniel P., and Gerald M. Weinberg
Handbook of Walkthroughs, Inspections, and Technical Reviews: Evaluating Programs, Projects, and Products, Third Edition

Graybeal, Wayne, and Udo W. Pooch
Simulation: Principles and Methods

Greenfield, S. E.
The Architecture of Microcomputers

Greenwood, Frank
Profitable Small Business Computing

Healy, Martin, and David Hebditch
The Microcomputer in On-Line Systems: Small Computers in Terminal-Based Systems and Distributed Processing Networks

Lemone, Karen A., and Martin E. Kaliski
Assembly Language Programming for the VAX-11

Lias, Edward J.
Future Mind: The Microcomputer—New Medium, New Mental Environment

Lines, M. Vardell, and Boeing Computer Services Company
Minicomputer Systems

Marca, David
Applying Software Engineering Principles

Mashaw, B. J.
Programming Byte by Byte: Structured FORTRAN 77

Mills, Harlan D.
Software Productivity

Monro, Donald M.
Basic BASIC: An Introduction to Programming

Mosteller, William S.
Systems Programmer's Problem Solver

Nickerson, Robert C.
COBOL Programming

Nickerson, Robert C.
Fundamentals of FORTRAN Programming

Nickerson, Robert C.
Fundamentals of Programming in BASIC

Parikh, Girish
Techniques of Program and System Maintenance

Parkin, Andrew
Data Processing Management

Parkin, Andrew
Systems Analysis

Pizer, Stephen M., with Victor L. Wallace
To Compute Numerically: Concepts and Strategies

Pooch, Udo W., William H. Greene, and Gary G. Moss
Telecommunications and Networking

Reingold, Edward M., and Wilfred J. Hansen
Data Structures

Savitch, Walter J.
Abstract Machines and Grammars

Schneiderman, Ben
Software Psychology: Human Factors in Computer and Information Systems

Simpson, Tom, and Shaffer & Shaffer Applied Research & Development, Inc.
VisiCalc® Programming: No Experience Necessary

Shaffer & Shaffer Applied Research & Development, Inc.
VisiCalc® Programming: No Experience Necessary for the Apple® II, II Plus, and IIe Personal Computers

Shaffer & Shaffer Applied Research & Development, Inc.
VisiCalc® Programming: No Experience Necessary for the ATARI® 800™ and 1200XL™ Home Computers

Shaffer & Shaffer Applied Research & Development, Inc.
VisiCalc® Programming: No Experience Necessary for the IBM® Personal Computer

Shaffer & Shaffer Applied Research & Development, Inc.
VisiCalc® Programming: No Experience Necessary for the TRS-80® Model III Microcomputer

Walker, Henry M.
Problems for Computer Solutions Using FORTRAN

Walker, Henry M.
Problems for Computer Solutions Using BASIC

Weinberg, Gerald M.
Rethinking Systems Analysis and Design

Weinberg, Gerald M.
Understanding the Professional Programmer

Weinberg, Gerald M., Stephen E. Wright, Richard Kauffman, and Martin A. Goetz
High Level COBOL Programming

BASIC for IBM®
Personal Computers

Harriet Morrill

Little, Brown and Company
Boston   Toronto

Library of Congress Cataloging in Publication Data

Morrill, Harriet.
  BASIC for IBM personal computers.

  (Little, Brown computer systems series)
  Includes index.
    1. IBM Personal Computer—Programming. 2. Basic
(Computer program language) I. Title. II. Title:
B.A.S.I.C. for I.B.M. personal computers. III. Series.
QA76.8.I2594M67   1984   001.64′24   83-19956
ISBN 0-316-58402-9

Library of Congress Catalog Card No. 83-19956

ISBN 0-316-58402-9

9   8   7   6   5   4   3   2   1

HAL

Published simultaneously in Canada
by Little, Brown & Company (Canada) Limited

Printed in the United States of America

IBM is a registered trademark of International Business Machines Corporation.

Disclaimer of Liabilities: Due care has been exercised in the preparation of this book to insure its effectiveness. The author and publisher make no warranty, expressed or implied, with respect to the programs or other contents of this book. In no event will the author or publisher be liable for direct, indirect, incidental, or consequential damages in connection with or arising from the furnishing, performance, or use of this book.

for Jim, Molly, and Jimmy

Preface

BASIC for IBM® Personal Computers is, first and foremost, a guide to learning BASIC. It carries you, regardless of your math background and computing experience, from the beginning of programming through the use of data files, graphics, music, and color.

This book works for all of the computers in the IBM personal computer family because, although each IBM personal computer has features designed for a particular computing environment, they all share a common computer technology. For example, the IBM PC XT includes extensive disk storage capacity and can easily be expanded. The IBM PCjr has less storage and expansion facilities but can accept pre-written programs in cartridge form, and its keyboard need not be attached by a cord. All of the IBM personal computers, however, share the same microprocessor (8088) and the same start-up version of BASIC, cassette BASIC. If it does not have it originally, any IBM personal computer can be configured to include the disk operating system (DOS) and Advanced BASIC. Thus, they all have the potential to take advantage of any of the BASIC language features described in *BASIC for IBM Personal Computers*.

Parts One and Two of this book teach you to write programs using the universal BASIC statements. They also describe the components of a computer system and explain how computers work. The remaining sections cover the more powerful BASIC statements, data files, and the special features of IBM personal computers. The computer dating project illustrates the entire programming process from program design to program execution.

The only equipment you need to start learning BASIC with this book is an IBM personal computer (with any amount of RAM) and a TV monitor. If you have a disk (fixed or floppy), this book explains the BASIC statements that use the disk for data file processing. If you have a color display and adapter, it explains BASIC statements that use the spectacular color facilities. *BASIC for IBM Personal Computers* also describes statements that make use of the printers, graphics, and music components that can be included in any IBM personal computer system.

The easiest way to find out which features your computer has is by trying them out. Try what *BASIC for IBM Personal Computers* says and see if it works for you — you can't hurt your computer! You are most likely to notice differences if you are using the entry model of the IBM PCjr. The PCjr keyboard has only 62 keys; the others have 83. This is no problem, though, because all of the same keyboard functions can be accomplished on the PCjr by using a combination of keys. The PCjr has a game, Keyboard Adventure, which explains the keys and their functions. The print line on the entry model PCjr has only 40 characters; the print line for the other IBM personal computers has 80 characters. On the other hand, the IBM PCjr has a few music and color statements the others do not have. The BASIC Language Reference Manual that comes with your computer gives details on all of the available BASIC statements.

IBM personal computers and BASIC, the programming language this book explains, are both products of an historical force: the drive to bring computing to everyone. Early computers were enormous, fragile, and extremely expensive to build and maintain; they were also very difficult to program. Their first use was to support the military operations of World War II.

During the 1950s, IBM made important breakthroughs by adapting this new technology to business uses. In the mid-1960s, at Dartmouth College, John Kemeny and Thomas Kurtz developed BASIC (Beginner's All-purpose Symbolic Instruction Code) as a language so similar to ordinary English that they hoped it would make programming quite easy. Then, the theory went, having mastered BASIC first, programmers would quickly be able to learn the more complex languages of the real computing world.

It is no longer a matter of learning BASIC to get started. People learn BASIC to arm themselves with a valuable lifetime skill. Since the 1960s many computer manufacturers and computer scientists have contributed to the effort to produce computers that are smaller, more durable, and easier-to-program. Programmers have embellished BASIC so that its use has gone beyond the classroom to become the primary language of the mini- and microcomputers used in many homes and businesses.

IBM personal computers incorporate all of these efforts. In terms of accessibility, speed, durability, and capacity, the equipment has dramatically advanced since the 1940s. In its carrying case, the IBM PCjr can fit under an airline passenger seat! The version of BASIC for the IBM personal computers includes capabilities for color graphics and music that were not even considered for the original Dartmouth BASIC.

BASIC for IBM Personal Computers embodies the fruits of many years of teaching and incorporates the philosophy that the most effective learning is *active* learning. It deliberately presents the INPUT statement and character string data, the most interesting beginning aspects of programming, at the outset; it then follows with the usual mathematical operations and functions. The examples and exercises in the text and the Instructor's Manual have been tested on the high school level at The Hotchkiss School in Lakeville, Connecticut, and on the university level at Wesleyan University in Middletown, Connecticut.

BASIC for IBM Personal Computers is a companion to my book, *Mini and Micro BASIC* (Little, Brown and Company, Boston, 1983), which explains BASIC for the APPLE, TRS-80, and PDP-11 computers. The chapter exercises are the same for both books. Thus, any teaching environment that includes all four types of computers, or a combination of some of them, can have consistent assignments using both books.

Several people have contributed to making this a rigorous but cheerful book. Russ Walter, Director of the Wesleyan University Summer Computer Institute and author of *The Secret Guide to Computers*, has shared unsparingly his vast technical knowledge. For several years and many projects, Anne Bartram has done *all* of the secretarial tasks with intelligence and patience. Ron and Sara O'Connor have contributed their cheerfulness. And my family, James Martin, James Arthur, and Molly MacKenzie Morrill, have made the sacrifices and provided the discipline and humor needed to see such a project through to completion.

Harriet Morrill
Lakeville, 1983

Contents

Part Two   Cornerstones

Part Three   Commonly Used Features

BASIC for IBM® Personal Computers

Part One

Fundamentals

Chapter 1

A Sample Computing Session

The best way to learn to program in BASIC is by trial and error. So, if you're stretched out in some cozy place, pick up your book and go find a computer. You may not be quite as comfortable there, but you will feel a great sense of accomplishment as you work through the illustrations in this chapter. Type them into your computer and take a few minutes to be sure you understand what they do. Before you finish your first session, make up an example of your own.

As a programmer, your job is to enter into the computer a program of BASIC language instructions for solving a problem. The computer's job is to translate your program into its own electronic language and then to carry out each instruction. Thus, your first task when you sit down to work is to activate the BASIC language translator.

Beginning BASIC requires no computer disks; just close any open disk drive doors. Then turn on the display screen, turn on the computer, and wait for the OK prompt to appear.

The OK prompt tells you that the computer is set for BASIC. Thus, if you want it to calculate how long it took to build the Brooklyn Bridge, you should gather the information needed and type the BASIC program in Illustration 1.1 into the computer. Press the CAPS LOCK key to simplify your typing by using all capitals, copy the spaces as well as the characters, and remember to press ↵ , for enter, at the end of each line.

ILLUSTRATION 1.1

A computer program written in BASIC

```
10 PRINT "THE BROOKLYN BRIDGE"
20 PRINT "STARTED IN 1898 AND FINISHED IN 1910"
30 PRINT "IT TOOK"
40 PRINT 1910-1898
50 PRINT "YEARS TO BUILD"
60 END
```

When you enter the command RUN the computer will begin by obeying your first instruction; then it will follow the sequence of line numbers. You will see:

```
RUN

THE BROOKLYN BRIDGE
STARTED IN 1898 AND FINISHED IN 1910
IT TOOK
 12
YEARS TO BUILD
```

Notice the position of number 12. The computer surrounds numbers that are not within quotes with a leading space for a minus sign and a trailing space.

Corrections

Correct your program by retyping any of the lines. For example, type:

```
20 PRINT "STARTED IN 1870 AND FINISHED IN 1883"
40 PRINT 1883-1870
```

and then RUN your program:

```
THE BROOKLYN BRIDGE
STARTED IN 1870 AND FINISHED IN 1883
IT TOOK
 13
YEARS TO BUILD
```

Or, add to your program by typing a new line with a number that will be inserted into the sequence:

```
25 PRINT "WORK WAS DANGEROUS AND SLOW"
```

RUN the program now:

```
THE BROOKLYN BRIDGE
STARTED IN 1870 AND FINISHED IN 1883
WORK WAS DANGEROUS AND SLOW
IT TOOK
 13
YEARS TO BUILD
```

To erase a line enter its number with nothing after it.

As you work, your screen may become a hodgepodge of rewritten and retyped lines:

```
10 PRINT "THE BROOKLYN BRIDGE"
20 PRINT "STARTED IN 1898 AND FINISHED IN 1910"
30 PRINT "IT TOOK"
40 PRINT 1910-1898
50 PRINT "YEARS TO BUILD"
60 END
20 PRINT "STARTED IN 1870 AND FINISHED IN 1883"
40 PRINT 1883-1870
25 PRINT "WORK WAS DANGEROUS AND SLOW"
```

To clear the screen, type CLS or press the CTRL and HOME keys simultaneously. Then, to see whether the computer has correctly interpreted your changes, type LIST. It will present the current (latest) version of your program. In Illustration 1.2, lines 20 and 40 were rewritten and line 25 was inserted.

ILLUSTRATION 1.2

The LIST command shows the program with the changes.

```
LIST

10 PRINT "THE BROOKLYN BRIDGE"
20 PRINT "STARTED IN 1870 AND FINISHED IN 1883"
25 PRINT "WORK WAS DANGEROUS AND SLOW"
30 PRINT "IT TOOK"
40 PRINT 1883-1870
50 PRINT "YEARS TO BUILD"
60 END
```

Program Format

The bridge program in Illustration 1.2 is a complete BASIC computer program. It has numbered instructions, each of which is written in the following form:

| Line number | — | BASIC keyword | — | Blank space | — | Programmer's data if needed |

The BASIC statements that this program illustrates are the PRINT statement, which tells the computer to print the data on the user's terminal, and the END statement, which tells the computer where the program ends. There are about 10 standard statements that form the cornerstones of the BASIC language. Even though they are quite simple to use, they are powerful enough to make the computer perform very complicated tasks.

There are also many more sophisticated BASIC statements. Many of these combine the functions of several statements into one, so that it takes fewer of them to accomplish the same tasks. Other statements serve to activate equipment not found in all computer systems. The statements to create graphics designs in the IBM personal computer's version of BASIC are examples of this.

The PRINT Statement

As you can see from the bridge program, the PRINT statement is a powerful tool. It tells the computer to print messages, as in line 10, or it tells the computer to do a calculation such as the subtraction 1883 − 1870 in line 40. Even more, a single PRINT statement can do several of these jobs. Illustration 1.2 can be shortened by erasing lines 40 and 50 and replacing the existing line 30 with a new line 30:

```
50                                                      (erase line 50)
40                                                      (erase line 40)
30 PRINT "IT TOOK";1883-1870;"YEARS TO BUILD"    (rewrite line 30)
```

LIST the program to see the whole current version:

```
LIST

10 PRINT "THE BROOKLYN BRIDGE"
20 PRINT "STARTED IN 1870 AND FINISHED IN 1883"
25 PRINT "WORK WAS DANGEROUS AND SLOW"
30 PRINT "IT TOOK";1883-1870;"YEARS TO BUILD"
60 END
```

RUN the program:

```
RUN

THE BROOKLYN BRIDGE
STARTED IN 1870 AND FINISHED IN 1883
WORK WAS DANGEROUS AND SLOW
IT TOOK 13 YEARS TO BUILD
```

The semicolons tell the computer that there is more than one field of data to be printed. They also direct the computer to print the successive fields one right after another on the same line.

If line 30 of the bridge program was:

```
30 PRINT "IT TOOK", 1883-1870, "YEARS TO BUILD"
```

with commas instead of semicolons, a RUN would look like this:

```
THE BROOKLYN BRIDGE
STARTED IN 1870 AND FINISHED IN 1883
WORK WAS DANGEROUS AND SLOW
IT TOOK           13                YEARS TO BUILD
```

The computer sees a line of printing as being divided into print zones of 14 characters each. Commas in the PRINT statement tell the computer to print the next item of data in the next print zone on the line. They are used mainly to set up tables of information with neat-looking columns, as in Illustration 1.3. Notice line 20. A PRINT statement with no specific data causes the computer to print a blank line, which is a convenient way to separate headings from the body of data.

ILLUSTRATION 1.3

Commas in PRINT produce columns for tables of information.

```
10 PRINT "NAME","PHONE"
20 PRINT
30 PRINT "MICKEY","333-1313"
40 PRINT "LUCY","245-1987"
50 PRINT "MOLLY","657-3434"
60 END

RUN

NAME        PHONE

MICKEY      333-1313
LUCY        245-1987
MOLLY       657-3434
```

The LPRINT Statement

If your computer has a printer, turn it on and use LPRINT in place of PRINT to have results printed on paper as your program RUNs. To produce a printed copy of the Brooklyn Bridge report the example program becomes:

```
10 LPRINT "THE BROOKLYN BRIDGE"
20 LPRINT "STARTED IN 1870 AND FINISHED IN 1883"
25 LPRINT "WORK WAS DANGEROUS AND SLOW"
30 LPRINT "IT TOOK";1883-1870;"YEARS TO BUILD"
60 END
```

Type LLIST to have a copy of your program listed by the printer. It's always a good idea to keep "hard copy" versions of the programs you write.

The WIDTH Statement

```
10 WIDTH 40
```

sets printing for 40 large characters on a line. If you use commas to separate items when WIDTH 40 is in effect, there are only two 14 character print zones.

```
10 WIDTH 80
```

sets printing for 80 narrow characters and five print zones per line. The first four zones have 14 characters each, the last has 10 characters.

WIDTH 80 is the start-up print setting. If you wish to change it, include the WIDTH statement in your program before your PRINT statements.

The COLOR Statement

The COLOR statement sets the hues of the display screen. It allows you to specify colors for the characters (foreground), the background, and a border:

```
5 COLOR 14,9,4
```

In this line 5, the first color number, 14, represents the foreground. It is 14, for yellow. The second number represents the background. Nine stands for blue. The third color, 4, or red, will be the border color. Illustration 1.4 is a list of all of the available colors and the rules for using them.

ILLUSTRATION 1.4

Display color codes for the IBM personal computer
with the color/graphics monitor adapter

0 Black	8 Gray
1 Blue	9 Light blue
2 Green	10 Light green
3 Cyan	11 Light cyan
4 Red	12 Light red
5 Magenta	13 Light magenta
6 Brown	14 Yellow
7 White	15 High-intensity white

1. The foreground colors may be from 0 to 31. That is, colors 0 to 15; but you may add 16 to any number to make characters blink in that color.
2. The background may be from 0 to 7.
3. The border may be from 0 to 15.

If you wish to set some of these colors but not others, omit a number, but insert a comma to represent its position. To set a red border, type:

```
5 COLOR , ,4
```

The positions you skip keep their current color. To turn off color and return to a black and white display, type:

```
COLOR 7,8
```

while you are working. Or, include it as the last line of a program you will RUN:

```
999 COLOR 7,8
```

The colors that are available on the IBM personal computer are spectacular, but to make use of them you need a color monitor or TV and a color/graphics adapter inserted in the computer. If you have a black and white screen and the monochrome adapter, your choices are still interesting but limited. Illustration 1.5 lists them.

Regardless of the computer equipment you have, keep experimenting with COLOR and other display features. The displays you create are advertisements for all the good computing work that lies behind the scenes.

ILLUSTRATION 1.5

Display color codes for the IBM personal computer without color equipment

Foreground	Background
0 Black	0 Black
1 White, underlined	7 White
7 White	
15 High-intensity white	

Writing Your Own Program

Now is the time to write your own program. You will find the most difficult part of the project is using the unfamiliar keyboard. If you make an error, correct it by retyping the line.

Begin by entering the NEW command to clear the computer of other work. Then enter your program line by line, pressing ↵ at the end of each one. Keep track of your work with the LIST command and, finally, give the RUN command. Wrap up your computing session by turning off both the screen and the computer. If you are using a computer with a disk and wish to save this first program, the section called "Using the Diskette" in Chapter 2 explains what to do.

Problems

Programming problems

1. Commands are instructions given without line numbers in response to the OK prompt. They tell the computer how to manipulate your BASIC program. In the lines on the left, write the commands to perform the functions given in the sentences below:

   a. _____ Clear storage of previous work and prepare to accept a new program.

   b. _____ Display the current version of your program on the screen.

   c. _____ Print the current version of your program on the printer.

   d. _____ Execute the program currently in storage.

2. Enter the program in Illustration 1.2 and change it to report the construction time of the George Washington Bridge, which was begun in 1927 and finished in 1931.

3. Enter the program in Illustration 1.2 and change it to report the time span between the publication of Darwin's *Origin of the Species* and the confirmation of Einstein's general theory of relativity. Darwin's book was published in 1859 and the general theory was proven true in 1922.

Programs to write

4. Write a program to calculate and print out the age of Mickey Mouse when you were born. Mickey was "born" in 1929.

5. Write a program that produces the following table of English–metric conversions.

English	Metric
1 inch	2.54 centimeters
1 mile	1.609 kilometers
1 pound	453.6 grams

6. The race around the lake started at noon. Have the computer calculate and print the times of the first three finishers. They finished at 12:21, 12:23 and 12:42, respectively. Label your output.

7. Jimmy sent away for Boy Scout camp gear. The items cost $42.50 plus $6.38 sales tax and $1.80 postage. Have the computer calculate and print the total that Jimmy must pay. Label the output. (Do *not* enter the dollar sign, "$"; its special use will be explained later.)

8. The high temperature for the day was 61°F. The low was 38°F. Have the computer calculate and print the extent of the temperature change during the 24-hour period. Label the output.

9. Use the computer to tally the total income received by the Winter Ski Jump Association from the winter carnival. The proceeds from the various sources were:

Tickets	$500.00
Refreshments	150.00
Programs	75.00

If the association spent 100 dollars for judges, what was its profit? Label the output.

Corrections

10. In the spaces on the right, write "Correct" if the following BASIC statements are correctly entered. If not, rewrite them correctly. Consider each statement separately. These statements are not part of the same program.

    a. 15 PRINT A; "IS CORRECT" _____

    b. 55 PRINT X; IS THE SOLUTION _____

    c. 28 PRINT "Y"; IS NOT THE SOLUTION _____

    d. 10 PRINT "YOUR NAME" _____

    e. 5 PRINT YOUR AGE _____

    f. 52 PRINT _____

    g. END _____

    h. 50 RUN _____

    i. END PRINT _____

    j. "PRINT YOUR ANSWER" _____

Chapter 2

A Closer Look at Your Computer System

"Computer system" rather than "computer" best describes the equipment you are using. It is really a network of components and concepts that has emerged from technological history. This chapter describes the codes and devices that form the cornerstones of a computer system and explains how they affect you as a programmer.

Software

The calculating and other miracles accomplished by computers occur because computers use speedy, precise electrical circuits to express numbers and characters rather than the cumbersome marks of a pen, the beads of an abacus, or the mechanical gears of various devices used by preceding generations. The genius of computer scientists has been to combine the properties of electrical energy with the notion of the binary number system and to build upon the fundamental concept that one electrical impulse should signal one binary digit. They have gone on to establish that combinations of binary digits can signify numbers, alphabetic characters, or even logical concepts such as true or false.

The resulting electric computer codes are the Indian smoke signals and talking drumbeats of modern civilization. Known as *software,* over the years they have become so sophisticated that they are considered whole languages.

BASIC, the language we are talking about, is one of several high-level computer languages that produce electrical representations of your ideas. COBOL (*CO*mmon *B*usiness *O*riented *L*anguage), as its name implies, is used for business data processing; it is the most widely used computer language. FORTRAN (*FOR*mula *TRAN*slation), used for scientific projects, was the first important computer language. PASCAL has recently become more popular because it makes it easy to write programs using good programming style.

The Binary Number System

The binary number system is the link between the world of humans and the world of machines that makes computing possible. This number system is so fundamental to computing that it is worthwhile to take time to review its characteristics.

Like the familiar decimal system, it is a code for expressing numerical amounts. And like all place-value number systems, it requires two operations: selecting the correct digit and placing it in the appropriate column.

The decimal system uses ten digits: 0, 1, 2, 3, 4, 5, 6, 7, 8, 9. The binary uses two: 0, 1. The columns of the decimal system represent powers of ten. The columns of the binary system represent powers of two. From right to left, the first four columns of these systems are shown in Illustration 2.1.

ILLUSTRATION 2.1

Place values in the decimal and binary number systems

	Decimal				Binary		
. . .	10^3	10^2	10^1	10^0	. . .	2^3	2^2	2^1	2^0
. . .	Thousands	Hundreds	Tens	Ones	. . .	Eights	Fours	Twos	Ones

Placing a digit in a column declares how many times you intend to count the quantity represented by the column. Illustration 2.2 compares the way one dozen is expressed in each system. Write one dozen in the decimal system with a one in the tens column and a two in the ones column: 12. Express one dozen in the binary system with a one in the eights column, and a one in the fours column. Place zero in the twos and ones columns: 1100. These right-hand zeros are necessary to show which columns are represented with ones, the significant digits. Since you know what the column positions and digits stand for in each system, you know that 12 in decimal expresses the same as 1100 in binary.

ILLUSTRATION 2.2

Expressing one dozen in decimal and binary

		Decimal					Binary		
. . .	10^3	10^2	10^1	10^0	. . .	2^3	2^2	2^1	2^0
. . .	Thousands	Hundreds	Tens	Ones	. . .	Eights	Fours	Twos	Ones
. . .			1	2	. . .	1	1	0	0

Binary Codes

Bit is the computer term for binary digit. The two possible binary digits are easily expressed electrically, because electric circuits can be viewed as having two states: ON and OFF. Computer scientists have agreed that a circuit ON is ONE and a circuit OFF is ZERO. When circuits are arranged as columns of the binary system, numbers are represented. In Illustration 2.3, one dozen is signaled by energizing the proper circuits.

ILLUSTRATION 2.3

Expressing one dozen electrically

	2^3	2^2	2^1	2^0
• • •	The eights circuit	The fours circuit	The twos circuit	The ones circuit
• • •	On	On	Off	Off
	1	1	0	0

Imagine that you had millions of circuits, as some computers do. If each represented a column of the binary system, you could express any quantity you would ever want. In reality, computers do not use millions of circuits to represent a number. Computer scientists view bits in units of eight, called *bytes,* and set arbitrary limits as to the number of bytes a particular computer will reserve for representing a number. These limits determine both the range of numbers and the number of significant digits by which one is represented on any particular system.

To greatly expand the binary code's usefulness and create high-level languages, scientists invented a code known as the American

ILLUSTRATION 2.4

The American National Standard Code for Information Interchange

ASCII CODE*	Character	ASCII CODE*	Character	ASCII CODE*	Character	ASCII CODE*	Character
000	(null)	032	(space)	064	@	096	´
001	☺	033	!	065	A	097	a
002	☻	034	"	066	B	098	b
003	♥	035	#	067	C	099	c
004	♦	036	$	068	D	100	d
005	♣	037	%	069	E	101	e
006	♠	038	&	070	F	102	f
007	(beep)	039	'	071	G	103	g
008	(backspace)	040	(	072	H	104	h
009	(tab)	041	)	073	I	105	i
010	(line feed)	042	*	074	J	106	j
011	(home)	043	+	075	K	107	k
012	(form feed)	044	,	076	L	108	l
013	(carriage return)	045	-	077	M	109	m
014	♫	046	.	078	N	110	n
015	☼	047	/	079	O	111	o
016	▶	048	0	080	P	112	p
017	◀	049	1	081	Q	113	q
018	↕	050	2	082	R	114	r
019	‼	051	3	083	S	115	s
020	¶	052	4	084	T	116	t
021	§	053	5	085	U	117	u
022	▬	054	6	086	V	118	v
023	↨	055	7	087	W	119	w
024	↑	056	8	088	X	120	x
025	↓	057	9	089	Y	121	y
026	→	058	:	090	Z	122	z
027	←	059	;	091	[	123	{
028	(cursor right)	060	<	092	\	124	¦
029	(cursor left)	061	=	093	]	125	}
030	(cursor up)	062	>	094	∧	126	~
031	(cursor down)	063	?	095	–	127	⌂

* decimal system notation

ASCII CODE*	Character	ASCII CODE*	Character	ASCII CODE*	Character	ASCII CODE*	Character
128	Ç	160	á	192	└	224	α
129	ü	161	í	193	┴	225	β
130	é	162	ó	194	┬	226	Γ
131	â	163	ú	195	├	227	π
132	ä	164	ñ	196	─	228	Σ
133	à	165	Ñ	197	+	229	σ
134	å	166	a	198	╞	230	µ
135	ç	167	o	199	╟	231	τ
136	ê	168	¿	200	╚	232	Φ
137	ë	169	⌐	201	╔	233	-o-
138	è	170	¬	202	╩	234	Ω
139	ï	171	½	203	╦	235	δ
140	î	172	¼	204	╠	236	∞
141	ì	173	¡	205	═	237	φ
142	Ä	174	«	206	╬	238	∈
143	Å	175	»	207	╧	239	∩
144	É	176	░	208	╨	240	≡
145	æ	177	▒	209	╤	241	±
146	Æ	178	▓	210	╥	242	≥
147	ô	179	│	211	╙	243	≤
148	ö	180	┤	212	╘	244	⌠
149	ò	181	╡	213	╒	245	⌡
150	û	182	╢	214	╓	246	÷
151	ù	183	╖	215	╫	247	≈
152	ÿ	184	╕	216	╪	248	°
153	Ö	185	╣	217	┘	249	•
154	Ü	186	║	218	┌	250	·
155	¢	187	╗	219	█	251	√
156	£	188	╝	220	▄	252	n
157	¥	189	╜	221	▌	253	²
158	Pts	190	╛	222	▐	254	■
159	ƒ	191	┐	223	▀	255	(blank 'FF')

National Standard Code for Information Interchange (ASCII) that gives numerical equivalents for letters and characters. Each of these can be expressed in one byte. One form of the code, with the characters and their numerical equivalents, is listed in Illustration 2.4. Scientists have also defined binary equivalents for many concepts such as true and false, larger and smaller, addition and subtraction. In fact, the computer languages use such ingenious adaptations of the binary code that you will be able to code almost anything you wish to express.

The CHR$( ) Function

Even though you see only some of the ASCII characters on the keyboard, the IBM personal computer makes nearly all of them available to you. Use the CHR$( ) function in a PRINT statement by inserting the decimal equivalent of the code number for the character you wish to see:

```
10 PRINT "THE CHARACTER WITH CODE 2 IS ";CHR$(2)
20 PRINT "THE CHARACTER WITH CODE 6 IS ";CHR$(6)
30 PRINT "THE CHARACTER WITH CODE 7 IS ";CHR$(7)
40 END

RUN

THE CHARACTER WITH CODE 2 IS ☻
THE CHARACTER WITH CODE 6 IS ♠
THE CHARACTER WITH CODE 7 IS !surprise!
OK
```

RUN this program with these and other code numbers to see the special characters. As you work, try to make use of them to enliven your computer displays.

The LOCATE Statement

In the usual text (not graphics) display mode, the computer sees the display screen as having 25 lines numbered from 1 at the top to 25 at the bottom. Each line has up to 80 print positions starting at 1 on the left and ending with 80 on the right. The LOCATE statement allows you to position printing on the screen by giving its line and then the character position location.

```
10 LOCATE 12,40
```

moves the lighted cursor to the center of the screen: down 12 lines from the top and across 40 positions from the left. The next PRINTing that occurs will begin at the position of the cursor.

Experiment with the LOCATE statement by using it to display the Brooklyn Bridge Report upside down:

```
10 LOCATE 20,20
20 PRINT "THE BROOKLYN BRIDGE"
30 LOCATE 19,20
40 PRINT "STARTED IN 1870 AND FINISHED IN 1883"
```

```
50 LOCATE 18,20
60 PRINT "WORK WAS DANGEROUS AND SLOW"
70 LOCATE 17,20
80 PRINT "IT TOOK";1883-1870;"YEARS TO BUILD."
90 END
```

Hardware

The combination of devices that comprise the computer system you are using is known as *hardware*. It is the culmination of three long strands of human history: the need to *store vast amounts of data*, the search for a *fast calculating machine*, and the desire to do these things *automatically*.

Calculations are performed in the central processing unit (CPU). Today, millions of calculations can be done in one second, but they must be done one at a time. Thus, the CPU needs a scratch pad to hold partial and final results and to store the program with the next instructions to be processed. Random access memory (RAM), or main storage, is the term for this temporary storage place. Computers are frequently compared in terms of the amount of RAM. ROM, or read only memory, stores a minimal version of the BASIC language.

No matter how large a computer's RAM may be, this storage is not designed to hold large files of information. Also, because the RAM is erased each time a new program is run or the computer is shut off, the system must include a device for long-term storage of a user's programs and data files. Usually, magnetic tapes or disks serve this purpose. Tapes are less expensive, but disks are faster and more reliable.

Computers become automatic through computer programs. Once a program has been written, stored, and set into operation, data processing and problem solving can continue indefinitely. Program writers and program users communicate with the computer through input and output (I/O) devices. As you know, keyboards are input devices that allow data and programs to be entered into the RAM. Screens and printers present the computer's output.

Look at Illustration 2.5 to identify the components of the computer system you are using. Your work as a computer programmer will be much easier if you can visualize where each component is and how it connects with the others.

ILLUSTRATION 2.5

The components and connections of a computer system

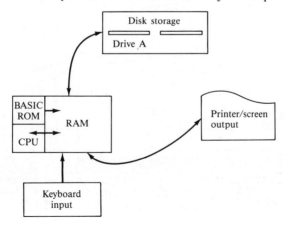

Look again at the position of the RAM in the diagram. This is the traffic center of the system. All input passes through the RAM to its destination: the CPU or long-term storage. All output passes from the CPU or storage device through the RAM to its destination: the screen or the printer.

Using the Diskette

The diskette that comes with the IBM personal computer already has many things stored on it. The DOS, or disk operating system, is a complex computer program that coordinates the communication among the various system components. The diskette also houses advanced BASIC language features. Illustration 2.6 shows how to get your IBM personal computer ready to work with a diskette.

ILLUSTRATION 2.6

Activating the BASIC diskette

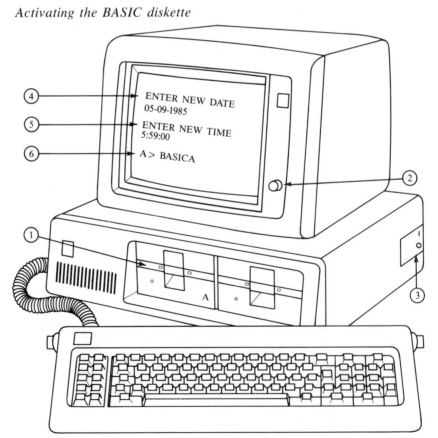

1. Insert a disk with IBM personal computer DOS into diskette drive A. Close the door.
2. Turn on the display screen.
3. Turn on the computer.
4. Enter the date as mm-dd-yy and ENTER ↵.
5. Enter the time as hh:mm;sec and press ENTER ↵.
6. Enter the command that requests the BASIC translator:

```
BASIC if you have Disk BASIC
BASICA if you have Advanced BASIC
```

(if you're not sure which version of BASIC you have, try both commands).

The process known as "booting the system" takes a minute, makes some whirring noises, and sets the red disk drive light on. Do not operate the disk drive while the light is on or you will harm your disk. Once the system is booted you can enter your programs at the keyboard, run them, and save them on the disk. Do this by thinking of a name from one to eight characters long, like MYFIRST. Enter SAVE "MYFIRST" and you will again see the disk light turn on. Once it goes out, your program has been

ILLUSTRATION 2.7

Saving a program on the diskette

```
OK
NEW
OK
10 PRINT "THE BROOKLYN BRIDGE"
20 PRINT "STARTED IN 1870 AND FINISHED IN 1883"
30 PRINT "IT TOOK"
40 PRINT 1883 - 1870
50 PRINT "YEARS TO BUILD"
60 END

RUN

THE BROOKLYN BRIDGE
STARTED IN 1870 AND FINISHED IN 1883
IT TOOK
 13
YEARS TO BUILD
OK
SAVE "MYFIRST"
OK
```

copied on the disk. When you are finished computing, remove your diskette and store it away from magnets, dust, smoke and rough handling.

Illustration 2.7 is a copy of what you would see on the screen if you were creating the first example in Chapter 1, the Brooklyn Bridge Report, and storing it on a disk. Words that are underlined are typed by the programmer; the others are printed by the computer. Remember to press ◄┘ after each line you type.

Tomorrow or next week, or whenever you choose, you can use your program again. First make sure that the disk on which it is stored is in the computer and that BASIC is active. Enter RUN "MYFIRST" and the computer will load a copy of the program into memory and proceed to do whatever you have programmed it to do.

ILLUSTRATION 2.8

IBM personal computer system commands

Command	Function
CLS	Clear the screen using the background color.
LIST	Display the program currently in RAM.
RENUM	Renumber the lines of the program in RAM starting at new line 10.
SAVE "MOLE"	Save a copy of the program in RAM on the disk.
LOAD "MOLE"	Bring a copy of the program on disk into RAM.
RUN "MOLE"	Load and execute the program on disk.
NAME "MOLE" AS "MOUSE"	Rename the program on disk.
KILL "MOLE"	Erase the program from the disk.
FILES	Display the directory of the disk.
Press CTRL and BREAK	Interrupt a program RUN and return to the OK prompt.
Press CTRL and NUM LOCK	Stop a program in the middle of a program RUN.
Press S (after CTRL/NUM LOCK)	Restart a program that has been stopped in the middle of a RUN.
Press CTRL, ALT and DEL	Reboot the disk.

Computer System Commands

Illustration 2.8 is a list of commands and keystrokes that will help you manipulate the programs you write. Give a command when the OK appears on the screen or include one in a program as a numbered statement. For example:

```
20 NAME "MYFIRST" AS "ORIGINAL"
```

Problems

Decimal-to-binary conversions

1. Convert each number from decimal to binary. Supply zeros to the left if necessary to make each an eight-bit number.

87_____   97_____

63_____   72_____

100_____   179_____

17_____   114_____

77_____   120_____

5_____   27_____

3_____   33_____

6_____   91_____

16_____   121_____

86_____   46_____

65_____   13_____

75_____   19_____

132_____   22_____

200_____   10_____

130_____   69_____

8_____   36_____

12_____   140_____

21_____   183_____

26_____   160_____

7_____   54_____

4_____   118_____

34_____   127_____

32_____   128_____

56_____

Binary-to-decimal conversions

2. Convert each number from binary to decimal.

100101_____   1001100_____

1000111_____   1100100_____

10111_____   1010100_____

10100_____   1111001_____

1111_____   10010011_____

1110_____   11100000_____

1010011_____   11010000_____

110011_____   110110_____

1011100_____   11011001_____

1101111_____   10_____

11000000_____	1001_____
10000111_____	101101_____
1000100_____	1011_____
10010010_____	11000_____
1100000_____	101010_____
110111_____	11001_____
10100011_____	110010_____
1110011_____	101110_____
10001010_____	10111110_____
1_____	11111011_____
10001_____	100011_____
11110_____	

Define the following terms:

3. Bit_____

4. Byte_____

5. ASCII_____

6. BASIC_____

7. FORTRAN_____

8. COBOL_____

Questions
9. Draw a diagram of a computer system. Label the components and show how they are connected.

10. Which three struggles in technological history led to the modern computer systems?

11. Explain what is meant by the statement "The binary number system is the link between the world of humans and the world of machines that makes computing possible."

12. How does the number of bytes a computer system uses to store a quantity affect the numbers that the system can represent?

13. Give the command which displays the directory of programs previously stored on the disk. Select a program and run it.

Part Two

Cornerstones

Chapter 3

Cornerstones of Data Processing

When the time to take the United States census for 1890 came near, officials realized that with the existing technology the results could not be tabulated before they became obsolete. The previous census, of 1880, was not tabulated before 1887!

The Census Bureau announced a competition to develop new methods for processing the 1890 data. Herman Hollerith, perhaps the world's first statistical engineer, won the competition with his invention of a system that used punched cards. His system greatly reduced the tabulating time. Hollerith's company eventually became a part of IBM, and his methods were absorbed into computer technology.

Because it is a fundamental reason for using computers, providing a means of storing information for later processing is an essential feature of a computer language. This chapter explains the LET, INPUT, and READ statements that form the cornerstone upon which BASIC's data processing facility is built. They let you temporarily store limited amounts of data. Later chapters explain how BASIC lets you permanently store larger data files on computer disks.

The LET Statement

The computer keeps track of the memory address where each item is stored. In BASIC, the LET statement is one way of assigning an address to a piece of information. Each time the address is referenced in a program, the data stored there is available for processing. In Illustration 3.1 the variables X, Y, and Z are symbols for the memory addresses for 1, 3, and 5, respectively.

ILLUSTRATION 3.1

LET assigns values to variables. PRINT displays the values assigned to a variable.

```
10 LET X=1     (storing data in X)
20 LET Y=3     (storing data in Y)
30 LET Z=5     (storing data in Z)
     .
     .
     .

100 PRINT "SOME ODD NUMBERS ARE:"
110 PRINT X, Y, Z     (referencing the data in X,Y,Z)
120 END

RUN

SOME ODD NUMBERS ARE:
 1        3        5
```

The LET statement can do calculations before assigning data to an address. Add these lines:

```
40 LET W = X+Y+Z

120 PRINT "THEIR SUM IS:"
130 PRINT W
140 END
```

Type LIST:

```
10 LET X = 1
20 LET Y = 3
30 LET Z = 5
40 LET W = X+Y+Z
100 PRINT "SOME ODD NUMBERS ARE:"
```

```
110 PRINT X, Y, Z
120 PRINT "THEIR SUM IS:"
130 PRINT W
140 END
```

Type RUN:

```
SOME ODD NUMBERS ARE:
 1        3        5
THEIR SUM IS:
 9
```

Each time a LET statement is executed, the expression on the right side of the equal sign (=) is evaluated. Because of the assignments in lines 10, 20, and 30, the right side of line 40 has the value 9. This value is then assigned to the storage location denoted by the variable (W) on the left side of the sign.

The equal sign in the LET statement is not at all like the one you've seen in algebra. In BASIC the two sides of the equal sign are *not* equivalent. It is not correct to say either LET X = 10 or LET 10 = X; only LET X = 10 will do. The term to the left of the sign must be a variable denoting a storage address. The right side may be a single value or a complicated expression denoting the data to be stored.

When you are used to writing LET statements, and it is clear to you that you are telling the computer to take whatever is on the right and store it in the location denoted by the variable on the left, leave the word LET out. Write X = 75 rather than LET X = 75. The equal sign tells the computer that this is a LET, or technically speaking, an assignment statement. Leave out LET and your life is a bit less complicated.

Some persons might also be mystified by the statement in this sample line 10:

```
10 X = X + 1
```

This looks like an equation that is out of balance, but it is actually a useful LET statement. The computer, in evaluating the right side first, adds 1 to the current value of X. (If none has been previously assigned, the computer assumes X to be zero.) The new value is stored back in location X, because it is the variable on the left. The previous X value has been erased. If X had been 1, it now would be 2. If the X = X + 1 statement is executed another time, the process is repeated. The computer is counting for you. X = X + 2 is the way to have the computer count by twos. X = X + 5 is a way to count by fives, and so on.

Character Strings and String Variables

Compare the two similar programs in Illustrations 3.2 and 3.3. As we have seen, Illustration 3.2 stores and prints numbers across the print line.

ILLUSTRATION 3.2

Storing numbers

```
10 LET X = 1
20 LET Y = 3
30 LET Z = 5
40 PRINT X,Y,Z
50 END
```

ILLUSTRATION 3.3

Storing characters

```
10 LET X$ = "SAM SMITH"
20 LET Y$ = "ELM ST."
30 LET Z$ = "542-2398"
40 PRINT X$,Y$,Z$
50 END
```

Running Illustration 3.3 produces:

```
SAM SMITH    ELM ST.    542-2398
```

It stores and prints character data, a facility that has greatly enhanced the usefulness of computers.

In BASIC, character data are known as string data to reflect the fact that they can consist of a "string" of any combination of up to 255 characters on the keyboard: letters, digits, punctuation marks, or any others. The computer stores string data in a more compact fashion than it stores numerical data, and the format of the variable and the strings themselves tell the computer to set this special character data-handling process in motion.

String variables must be concluded with $, as in X$. The character string itself must be surrounded with quotation marks, as in "SAM SMITH", except in some special situations where the data type is very clear. These situations will be explained as they are encountered, but you may feel that it is easier always to use quotation marks because it is never wrong to do so.

Choosing Variable Names

Variable names may be up to 40 characters long and can do a lot to make it easy to understand what your program does. They must begin with a letter and be followed by any letter of the alphabet, any digit, or a period (.).

The program:

```
10 Q = 5
20 P = .65
30 T = P * Q
```

can be written as:

```
10 QUANTITY.OF.COOKIES = 5
20 PRICE.PER.COOKIE = .65
30 TOTAL. = QUANTITY.OF.COOKIES * PRICE.PER.COOKIE
```

and its purpose is much clearer. In fact, using meaningful variable names is so helpful that doing so has become one of the required guidelines for professional programmers.

There are also disadvantages to consider. Long variable names use up computer storage. They are hard to retype correctly, and the computer views a misspelled variable as a completely different item. A good compromise would be to use variables of medium length, such as:

```
10 QUANTITY = 5
20 PRICE = .65
30 TOTAL = QUANTITY * PRICE
```

Use variable names of a similar length for strings as well. Write NAME$ rather than N$.

The INPUT Statement

This is the statement that allows you to enter information while a program is running. INPUT is why, contrary to popular myth, computers are likely to make life in our society more *personal*. Computer-driven manufacturing processes will adjust to individual preferences as each item is produced. We may all wear custom-made clothes. Your choice of size, color, and style will not be limited to a few predetermined averages. Someday you may enter your measurements into the pattern-cutting program of your local clothier's computer and, even if your jacket size differs from your skirt or pants size, you will be able to buy a suit that needs no alterations.

INPUT makes it possible for one program to process more than one set of data. For example, with INPUT there is no need to write several programs for calculating the construction time of several projects. As shown in Illustration 3.4, writing a single generalized program will do. As the program runs, the INPUT statement prompts the user to enter specific information.

ILLUSTRATION 3.4

INPUT allows you to enter data when the program runs.

```
10 PRINT "WHAT IS THE PROJECT"
20 INPUT P$
30 PRINT "WHEN WAS IT BEGUN"
40 INPUT B
50 PRINT "WHEN WAS IT FINISHED"
60 INPUT C
70 PRINT P$; "TOOK";C-B;"YEARS TO BUILD."
80 END
```

CUSTOM CLOTHING

Run the program and observe the effect of INPUT (the underlined words are typed and entered as the program runs).

```
RUN

WHAT IS THE PROJECT
? THE EMPIRE STATE BUILDING
WHEN WAS IT BEGUN
? 1926
WHEN WAS IT FINISHED
? 1931
THE EMPIRE STATE BUILDING TOOK 5 YEARS TO BUILD.
```

INPUT prints a question mark (?) to prompt the user to enter information. The computer stops execution at the INPUT statement and waits until something is entered. Then processing continues. In Illustration 3.4, three question marks appear because of the three INPUT statements, in lines 20, 40, and 60.

Data entered in response to the prompt are stored in the variables given in the INPUT statement. In Illustration 3.4, P$ becomes THE EMPIRE STATE BUILDING, B becomes 1926, and C becomes 1931. If these variables are referenced later in the program, as they are in line 70, the values entered are recalled.

Run the program again. New values can be entered and calculations performed using them:

```
WHAT IS THE PROJECT
? THE ANGKOR WAT
WHEN WAS IT BEGUN
? 1113
WHEN WAS IT FINISHED
? 1150
THE ANGKOR WAT TOOK 37 YEARS TO BUILD.
```

Only single constant values can be entered with an INPUT statement. Notice that a string variable, P$, is used to accept string data in Illustration 3.4. The string entered can be composed of any combination of characters, including blanks. The computer considers everything up to a comma, or everything within quotation marks, to be one string. Thus, if you wish to include a comma in a string, surround the string with quotation marks.

Any number may be entered for the numeric variables B or C in lines 40 and 60, but *commas, arithmetic expressions,* or *variables* may *not*. Thus, 4, or 4.5, or -12002345 is acceptable, but a variable such as A or an expression like $30 + 5,132$ is not allowed.

As with the PRINT statement, more than one job can be done in a single INPUT statement. Several values can be accepted, as in Illustration 3.5. Notice the responses are entered on one line, separated by commas.

ILLUSTRATION 3.5

A single INPUT assigns values to several variables.

```
10 PRINT "WEEKEND JOGGING TALLY"
20 PRINT "ENTER THE MILES FOR FRIDAY,SATURDAY,SUNDAY"
30 INPUT A,B,C
40 PRINT "YOU RAN A TOTAL OF";A+B+C;"MILES THIS WEEKEND."
50 END

RUN

WEEKEND JOGGING TALLY
ENTER THE MILES FOR FRIDAY,SATURDAY,SUNDAY
? 5, 5.3, 4
YOU RAN A TOTAL OF 14.3 MILES THIS WEEKEND.
```

The computer is satisfied if there are as many items entered as there are variables in the INPUT statement. If more are entered, or too few, the computer will respond with:

```
?REDO FROM START
```

and wait for you to enter all of your responses again.

On the IBM personal computer, INPUT has been enhanced to eliminate the need for a preceding PRINT statement to explain the prompt. You can write Illustration 3.6. This version of INPUT prints out the explanatory question and also the prompting question mark. Then it waits for a response.

ILLUSTRATION 3.6

INPUT " " prints messages and accepts values.

```
10 INPUT "WHAT IS YOUR PROJECT"; P$
20 INPUT "WHEN WAS IT BEGUN"; B
30 INPUT "WHEN WAS IT FINISHED"; C
40 PRINT P$;"TOOK";C-B;"YEARS TO BUILD."
50 END
```

```
RUN

WHAT IS YOUR PROJECT? MY FATHER'S HOUSE
WHEN WAS IT BEGUN? 1979
WHEN WAS IT FINISHED? 1981
MY FATHER'S HOUSE TOOK 3 YEARS TO BUILD.
```

The READ Statement and the DATA Statement

Often a computer project requires having standard information at hand: the months of the year, or the names of the players on the New York Yankees baseball team, for example. As the program executes, some or all of this information may be needed. It is provided by two statements, READ and DATA, as shown in Illustration 3.7. The statements are used in combination: DATA holds the information; READ accesses it.

ILLUSTRATION 3.7

READ assigns values to variables. DATA holds the values.

```
10 PRINT "THE SIZES OF THE SHIRTS WE SELL"
20 READ A$, B$, C$
30 PRINT "ARE ";A$;" AND ";B$;" AND ";C$
35 DATA SMALL, MEDIUM, LARGE
40 END

RUN

THE SIZES OF THE SHIRTS WE SELL
ARE SMALL AND MEDIUM AND LARGE
```

Think of an imaginary arrow that controls which item of data is assigned to which variable when the computer executes a READ statement. At the outset, the arrow aims at the first field of data, SMALL. This is assigned to the first variable in READ, A$. Then the arrow moves to MEDIUM and assigns it to the second variable, B$. Finally, the arrow moves on and LARGE is assigned to C$. Quite simply, each time a READ statement is encountered, the computer assigns data in a sequential manner. It begins using the data where the arrow has been set and continues until all of the READ variables have taken a value.

If there are fewer data fields than variables, the computer complains by printing "OUT OF DATA" and coming to a stop. If you have more data than the READ needs, there is no problem. In fact, as shown in Illustration 3.8, you may purposefully put the extra items in the DATA for use by another READ later in the program.

ILLUSTRATION 3.8

Several READ statements may appear in one program.

```
10  PRINT "THE SIZES OF THE SHIRTS WE SELL"
20  READ A$, B$, C$
30  PRINT "ARE ";A$;" AND ";B$;" AND ";C$
40  PRINT "BUT WE CAN MAKE"
50  READ D$
60  PRINT D$;" IF YOU NEED IT"
70  DATA SMALL, MEDIUM, LARGE, EXTRA LARGE
80  END

RUN

THE SIZES OF THE SHIRTS WE SELL
ARE SMALL AND MEDIUM AND LARGE
BUT WE CAN MAKE
EXTRA LARGE IF YOU NEED IT
```

Because of line 20 in Illustration 3.8, the arrow in DATA points to SMALL, MEDIUM, and LARGE and finally rests upon EXTRA LARGE. When READ occurs in line 50, the computer continues where the arrow indicates and assigns EXTRA LARGE to D$. The arrow has moved in the sequence shown in Illustration 3.9.

ILLUSTRATION 3.9

The imaginary arrow travels through DATA.

1. Before any READ statements:

   ```
   DATA SMALL, MEDIUM, LARGE, EXTRA LARGE
        ↑
   ```

2. After READ A$, B$, C$ in line 20:

   ```
   DATA SMALL, MEDIUM, LARGE, EXTRA LARGE
                             ↑
   ```

3. After READ D$ in line 50:

```
DATA SMALL, MEDIUM, LARGE, EXTRA LARGE
                                      ↑
```

Keeping the arrow in mind as you use the READ and DATA combination is important. DATA is a unique BASIC statement in that its line number does not matter. DATA needs a line number to fit into the general format of a BASIC program, but the position of the DATA statement in the program does not affect the sequence of events. READ determines which data will be used and when. Thus, Illustration 3.8 can be written as follows and the results are the same:

```
10 DATA SMALL, MEDIUM, LARGE, EXTRA LARGE
20 PRINT "THE SIZES OF THE SHIRTS WE SELL"
30 READ A$,B$,C$
40 PRINT "ARE ";A$;" AND ";B$;" AND ";C$
50 READ D$
60 PRINT "BUT WE CAN MAKE"
70 PRINT D$;" IF YOU NEED IT"
80 END
```

```
RUN

THE SIZES OF THE SHIRTS WE SELL
ARE SMALL AND MEDIUM AND LARGE
BUT WE CAN MAKE
EXTRA LARGE IF YOU NEED IT
```

The DATA statements could also be interspersed with other program statements with the same results:

```
10 PRINT "THE SIZES OF THE SHIRTS WE SELL"
20 DATA SMALL, MEDIUM, LARGE
30 READ A$, B$, C$
40 PRINT "ARE ";A$;" AND ";B$;" AND ";C$
50 DATA EXTRA LARGE
60 READ D$
70 PRINT "BUT WE CAN MAKE"
80 PRINT D$;" IF YOU NEED IT"
90 END

RUN

THE SIZES OF THE SHIRTS WE SELL
ARE SMALL AND MEDIUM AND LARGE
BUT WE CAN MAKE
EXTRA LARGE IF YOU NEED IT
```

Even if they are separated, the computer considers all of the data as belonging to one long list with the first datum in the lowest-numbered DATA statement at the top of the list and the last item in the highest-numbered DATA statement at the bottom.

Take a minute to notice the program data. The string constants like SMALL, MEDIUM, and LARGE have no quotation marks. DATA is one of the few places where quotation marks around string constants are not always needed. They can be used, of course, and they must be used if the string contains a comma, colons, or significant leading or trailing blanks.

READ, DATA, and the imaginary arrow work the same way for numbers as for strings. The only point to remember is that as with INPUT, numerical data must be a list of single values such as -10.6 or 8. Expressions like $5 + 5$ are not allowed.

Strings and numbers are often combined in READ and DATA statements. Take care to make sure the type of the variables in READ and the type of the corresponding data item match, as shown in Illustration 3.10.

ILLUSTRATION 3.10

The data types of the variables in READ match the values in DATA.

```
10 PRINT "A LIST OF PROJECTS AND CONSTRUCTION TIMES"
20 PRINT
30 READ A$,B
40 PRINT A$,B
50 READ C$,D
60 PRINT C$,D
70 READ E$,F
80 PRINT E$,F
90 DATA "BROOKLYN BRIDGE",13
100 DATA "ANGKOR WAT",37
110 DATA "FATHER'S HOUSE",3
120 END

RUN

A LIST OF PROJECTS AND CONSTRUCTION TIMES
BROOKLYN BRIDGE 13
ANGKOR WAT        37
FATHER'S HOUSE   3
```

The RESTORE Statement

As you use the READ and DATA combination, the imaginary arrow moves forward through the data. It never moves backward. RESTORE is a statement that moves the arrow back to the beginning of the data. Or, if you specify the line number of a DATA statement, RESTORE moves the arrow back to the first data item on the line. Once RESTORE has repositioned the arrow, any READing that follows starts from the new location of the arrow.

RESTORE is written quite simply as:

```
10 RESTORE   or   10 RESTORE 5
```

where 5 is the line number of a DATA statement.

ILLUSTRATION 3.11

RESTORE returns the arrow to the first item in DATA.

```
10 READ X
20 PRINT "THE FIRST PLACE TIME WAS";X;"MINUTES"
```

```
30 READ X
40 PRINT "THE SECOND PLACE TIME WAS";X;"MINUTES"
50 READ X
60 PRINT "THE THIRD PLACE TIME WAS";X;"MINUTES"
70 RESTORE
80 READ X
90 PRINT "THE WINNER BROKE THE RECORD BY"; 9-X; "MINUTES"
100 DATA 7,11,13
110 END

RUN

THE FIRST PLACE TIME WAS 7 MINUTES
THE SECOND PLACE TIME WAS 11 MINUTES
THE THIRD PLACE TIME WAS 13 MINUTES
THE WINNER BROKE THE RECORD BY 2 MINUTES
```

The first three READ statements in Illustration 3.11 move the arrow along the data. RESTORE in line 70 sets it back to the first data field, in this case to the 7. This is the value assigned to X in the READ statement, which follows in line 80.

Reminders for using READ, DATA, and RESTORE
1. The data type of the variable in READ must match the type of the data assigned to it.
2. READ statements may be, and usually are, interspersed with the rest of the program. All of the data need not be read at once.
3. There may be several DATA statements in a program. Even if they are separated, the computer considers all of the items as belonging to one long list.
4. DATA statements may occur anywhere in a program. Usually they appear at the very beginning or the very end as a way of separating the data from the body of the program.
5. DATA statements are an instance when quotation marks may not be needed around string constants.
6. Numbers in DATA statements must be single values, not arithmetic expressions.
7. RESTORE moves the arrow to the beginning of the data. The first READ following a RESTORE uses the first datum in the DATA statement indicated by the RESTORE statement.

Problems

Corrections

1. In the spaces on the right, write "Correct" if the following BASIC statements are correctly entered. If not, rewrite them as they should be. Consider each statement separately. These statements are not part of the same program.

   a. 90 READ _____

   b. 74 DATA _____

   c. 30 INPUT 1,3,5 _____

   d. 63 INPUT "HOW OLD ARE YOU ";F _____

   e. 40 DATA 45, 9–3, 2.6, 12–5 _____

   f. 99 INPUT A,B,C _____

   g. 90 DATA 3,2,.5,–7,2.5,1.2, –2 _____

   h. 58 INPUT _____

   i. 20 READ NAME, ADDRESS, PHONE _____

   j. 20 RESTORE 10 _____

   k. 77 INPUT YOUR NAME _____

   l. 5 LET "SUZY" = N$ _____

2. In the spaces on the right, write "Correct" if the following BASIC statements are correct. If not, rewrite them correctly. Consider each statement separately. These statements are not part of the same program.

   a. 60 DATA 4+5, 8, STATION #1, 1+2,2, STATION#2 _____

   b. 5 INPUT "YOUR NAME";A$ _____

   c. 10 READ A$,B$,C$
      34 DATA 314,"BASE HIT",45 _____

d. 20 READ "MY NAME" _____

e. 100 LET N = "JONES" _____

f. 12 INPUT A, B$, C _____

g. 77 LET A$ = MARY JONES _____

h. 44 DATA SUE, 89, FRED, 90, GIRLIE, 78 _____

i. 50 PRINT A$ = "MARY" _____

j. 72 PRINT "WHAT IS YOUR NAME";A$ _____

k. 44 READ "DATA" _____

l. 55 LET Y$ = "A VERY, VERY, LONG LINE OF INSTRUCTIONS"

3. If the following statements were part of a program, would they work properly? If not, state why not.

a. 10 READ A,X,B
   20 DATA 12
   30 DATA 4,5

b. 10 READ A,X,B
   20 DATA SUE, 9,20

c. 10 READ A,X,B
   20 DATA 12, 3

4. If the following pairs of BASIC statements were part of a program, would they work? If not, state why not.

a. 10 READ X$,A,B
   20 READ 9,20,70

b. 10 READ X$,Y$
   20 DATA ACE, BIG, CAT

c. 10 READ X$,A,B
   20 DATA 9,20,70

5. What will be printed when the following program is run?

```
10 LET A = 12
20 PRINT A
```

```
30  READ A,B
40  PRINT A+B
50  DATA 8,10
60  END
```

Programs to read

In the space on the right, write what will be printed when the following programs are run. If input from the terminal is needed, show some sample input that would fit the program.

```
6.  10 READ A
    20 READ B
    30 DATA 4,5,6,7,8,9
    40 RESTORE
    50 READ X,Y
    60 PRINT X;" PLUS ";Y;
    70 PRINT " IS "; X+Y
    80 END
```

```
7.  10 LET R$ = "MELANIE"
    20 LET X = 21
    30 PRINT "IS"
    40 PRINT R$
    50 PRINT X
    60 PRINT R$;" IS";X
    70 END
```

```
8.  10 PRINT "SALES OF MILK"
    20 PRINT
    30 READ A$,A
    40 PRINT A$,A
    50 GO TO 30
    60 DATA MONDAY,TUESDAY,WEDNESDAY,THURSDAY,FRIDAY
    70 DATA 25,26,32,42,38
    80 END
```

```
9.  10 READ M$
    20 READ B$
    30 DATA SHE
    40 RESTORE
    50 READ F$,J$,L$
    60 READ X$,Y$,Z$
    70 DATA "IS", " THE", WRITER
    80 READ P$,Q$,R$
```

```
90 DATA NOT, "THE", " TYPE"
100 DATA " HERE"
110 DATA ANYMORE
120 PRINT J$;L$;P$;X$;Q$
130 END
```

Programming problems

10. To reduce the federal deficit, social welfare programs will be cut by $15,275.80 each. The original budgets are:

    Health $42,756.99
    Education   84,546.50
    Welfare   92,250.00

    Use the computer to print out the new budget amounts and the total reduction in funds for these social programs. (Remember to omit the commas when entering these numbers.)

11. You are pursuing one of America's favorite pastimes, reading the label on your breakfast cereal box. It says:

    Percentage of U.S. Recommended Daily Allowances

	1 ounce of Dream Flakes
Protein	2
Vitamin A	25
Vitamin C	35
Iron	8

    You have eaten 2 ounces this morning. Use the computer to figure out what percentage of these nutrients you still need to consume today. Practice using the LET statement.

12. Write a program that asks for the year you were born. Have the computer print out the year you will retire and how many more years you must work before that date arrives.

13. The Altruism Foundation will match any donations made to the Scoville Library this year. Write a program that inquires about the amount of a donation and then prints out the total of the gift to the library after the donation has been matched.

14. Show how friendly the computer can be. Write a program that addresses the user by name. Ask him to enter one adverb, one noun, one adjective, and one verb. Print out a silly sentence using these words.

15. Write a program that stores the following data, reads them, and prints out the total of points scored for each hockey player along with his name. Print out the total points scored by the group.

Player's name	Points per period		
Marvin	1	0	0
Peter	2	2	1
Fred	1	1	1
Alan	2	0	1
Bill	0	1	1

16. Every registered voter in Democracy has been asked to phone two other voters in his or her precinct to ask them to register to vote in the upcoming election. Write a program that stores the following numbers of callers in each precinct and have it print out the total calls made in each. Also print out the grand total of phone calls.

Precinct	Registered voters
A	5,600
B	10,890
C	7,806
D	55,090
E	43,567

Chapter 4

Cornerstones of Calculations

At the beginning of the second century B.C., a computational problem was posed that was not solved for 2000 years. It begins:

> Compute, O friend, the host of the oxen of the sun, giving thy mind thereto, if thou hast a share of wisdom. Compute the number that once grazed upon the plains of the Sicilian Isle Trinacria and that were divided according to color into four herds, one milk white, one black, one yellow and one dappled.

The problem continues to state that there are more bulls than cows in each herd and to give nine other constraints. Then it concludes:

> When thou hast then computed the totals of the herd, O friend, go forth as a conqueror, and rest assured that thou art proved most skilled in the science of numbers.

In the nineteenth century a German mathematician concluded that the number of cattle was a 206,545-digit number beginning with 7766. Later in that century three men teamed up to carry on the computation. After four years they found 40 more digits.

It was not until 1965, when a computer was used, that all of the digits were determined. The problem was again solved in 1981 by a CRAY-1 computer in about 10 minutes, and all 206,545 digits were published in the *Journal of Recreational Mathematics*. At that time the CRAY-1 continued working and found five other numbers that satisfied all of the constraints. The largest of these has over a million digits!†

Computers are certainly prodigious calculators. Their speed and precision have greatly expanded our mathematical accomplishments. This is so even though the central processing unit, where calculations occur, is only one of several components in a computing system. Computers are data storage devices and automated problem solvers as well.

This chapter focuses on the computer's computational facility. It presents the cornerstone concepts you will need to take advantage of its computing tools: arithmetic operations and arithmetic functions.

Arithmetic Operations

In BASIC, the computer does all of the standard calculations using the following symbols:

^	for exponentiation
*	for multiplication
/	for division
\	for integer division
MOD	for modulo arithmetic
+	for addition
−	for subtraction

When more than one calculation occurs in an arithmetic expression, the computer scans the expression from left to right, doing exponentiation first, then either multiplication or division (whichever it encounters first), and finally either addition or subtraction. Thus, in a flash, the statement:

    10 PRINT 4 * 2 ^ 3+6 / 3 - 1

will be processed as:

Step one: $2 ^ 3 = 8$. Hence the computer stores:

    10 PRINT 4 * 8 + 6 / 3 - 1

Step two: $4 * 8 = 32$. Hence the computer stores:

    10 PRINT 32 + 6 / 3 - 1

---

†"Science and the Citizen," *Scientific American*, 245 (July 1981), 84.

Step three: 6 / 3 = 2. Hence the computer stores:

```
10 PRINT 32 + 2 - 1
```

Step four: 32 + 2 − 1 = 33. Hence the computer stores:

```
10 PRINT 33
```

Ultimately, 33 appears on the screen.

If you prefer to change this order of operations you can do so by surrounding the operation you wish to do first with parentheses. In the preceding example, if you wish to cube 4 * 2 rather than simply the 2, write:

```
10 PRINT (4 * 2) ^ 3+6 / 3 - 1
```

Step one would become 4 * 2 = 8, and the final outcome would be 513. When you write one set of parentheses inside another, the computer evaluates the inner parentheses first.

Use parentheses whenever you are not sure whether the computer will evaluate the expression as you wish. It is all right to use them even if they are unnecessary, and doing so often makes your meaning more clear.

Parentheses are usually helpful with fractions; certainly they are necessary when a fraction has a numerator or a denominator which includes an expression as:

$$\frac{6 + 8}{10 - 4}$$

In BASIC this becomes (6 + 8) / (10 − 4). Even with simple fractions, parentheses are a good idea, particularly if they are part of an expression. Thus $6\frac{1}{2}$ is more clearly presented as 6 + (1 / 2) than as 6 + 1 / 2.

A fractional exponent like $6^{1/3}$ *must* be written with parentheses as 6 ^ (1/3). If it is written 6 ^ 1 / 3 without parentheses, it will be evaluated as 6 ^ 1 divided by 3, or 2, rather than as the cube root of 6, which is 1.817121.

Integer division

The backslash operator tells the computer to round the operands to the nearest whole number before dividing and to truncate the decimals in the result. Thus,

```
10 PRINT 41.4 \ 3.6
```

becomes (in the computer)

```
10 PRINT 41/4
```

and the result is 10.1. Only the integer portion, the 10, is PRINTed.

Modulo arithmetic

The MOD operator performs the same integer division as the backslash but gives you the remainder portion of the result expressed as an integer. Thus,

```
10 PRINT 41.4 MOD 3.6
```

becomes

```
10 PRINT 41/4
```

and the result is 10.1. Only the remainder portion, the 1, is PRINTed.

Arithmetic Functions

Some arithmetic routines are so frequently used that they have been programmed right into the BASIC language. Known as arithmetic functions, they can be easily called into play by supplying the function name and your specific data. Function names are usually three-letter abbreviations, and data are usually written within parentheses. Use arithmetic functions in PRINT, LET, and all of the same situations as the usual arithmetic operations.

SQR

```
10 PRINT SQR(25)
20 END

RUN

5
```

SQR is the function name for square root; 25 is known as the argument; 5, the square root of 25, is called the function result.

Each computer has a unique group of functions supplied in its version of BASIC. As a programmer, you should acquaint yourself with the functions available on your system. They are listed in the IBM BASIC language manual.

Aside from SQR, there are three other very useful functions found in IBM personal computer BASIC: ABS, INT, and RND. They are presented here.

ABS

```
10 PRINT ABS(-1.7)
20 END

RUN

1.7
```

ABS is the function name for absolute value; −1.7 is the argument. The unsigned 1.7, which is the value of the argument without a sign, is the function result.

INT

```
10 PRINT INT(1.7)
20 END

RUN

1
```

```
 ─────┼────┼────┼────┼────┼────┼────┼────┼────┼─────
 −∞    ...   −2  −1.5  −1  −.5   0   +.5  +1  +1.5 +2   ...   +∞
```

INT is the function name for integer, a routine that *rounds the argument down* to the nearest *lower* integer. Imagine a continuum of all of the numbers from minus infinity to plus infinity. The INT of any number gives the nearest integer to the left on the continuum. Look at the continuum and you will see that:

The INT(1.5)   is: 1
The INT(.5)   is: 0
The INT(− .5)   is: − 1
The INT(2)   is: 2
The INT(0)   is: 0

To round off (up) as we usually do, add .5 to the argument (Illustration 4.1). Now the computer rounds up numbers that are at least halfway toward the next highest integer, and rounds down those close to the next lowest integer.

ILLUSTRATION 4.1

Using INT to round up

Number to be rounded	BASIC statement	Computer's interpretation	Final output
1.7	10 PRINT INT(1.7 + .5)	10 PRINT INT(2.2)	2
1.5	10 PRINT INT(1.5 + .5)	10 PRINT INT(2)	2
1.3	10 PRINT INT(1.3 + .5)	10 PRINT INT(1.8)	1

RND

```
10 PRINT RND
20 END

RUN

.541462
```

RND is the function name for the random-number generating function. The decimal .541462 is a sample RND result. It's an unpredictable number, between 0 and 1, that is calculated by the computer.

Frequently a random number is just what is needed, but a decimal of six digits or more is hardly useful. Who wants to play a guessing game for the secret number between 0 and 10 if a number like .345463 is a possible answer? Fortunately, it's not difficult to make the random decimal more useful. To transform it to an integer from 1 to 10, multiply by 10 to move the decimal one place to the right: 10 * RND. Then use INT to truncate the remaining decimals: INT(10*RND). Add 1 to make sure the number you have produced is not zero. Your BASIC statement would be:

```
10 PRINT INT(10*RND) + 1
```

Illustration 4.2 shows how these steps will affect some sample random decimals. Depending on which sample decimal is created by RND, executing the statement 10 PRINT INT (10*RND) + 1 will produce 1, 4, or 10.

To produce an integer within any range, apply the formula below to the RND function. If H is the highest number in the range and L is the lowest, write:

```
10 PRINT INT((H–L+1) * RND + L)
```

ILLUSTRATION 4.2

Transforming a random decimal to an integer between one and ten

	Sample decimal		
	.004366	*.345463*	*.999874*
1. Multiply by 10: 10*RND	.04366	3.45463	9.99874
2. Truncate decimals: INT(10*RND)	0	3	9
3. Add 1, the lowest number of the range you want: INT(10*RND)+1	1	4	10

This says: multiply the random decimal by the number of numbers in the range and add the lowest number in the range to the result.

Illustration 4.3 uses the random number function to stimulate the toss of a pair of dice.

ILLUSTRATION 4.3

Using RND to roll dice

```
10 PRINT "DICE TOSS"
20 PRINT INT(6 * RND) + 1
30 PRINT "AND"
40 PRINT INT(6 * RND) + 1
60 END

RUN

DICE TOSS
4
AND
2
```

Each time you run this program 4 and 2 will appear. To produce another sequence of numbers, add a negative argument to the RND function. As shown in Illustration 4.4, this changes the computer's "seed" number.

ILLUSTRATION 4.4

Using a negative argument for RND

```
10 INPUT "GIVE ME A STARTING VALUE"; N
20 PRINT "DICE TOSS"
30 PRINT INT(6 * RND(-N) ) + 1
```

```
40 PRINT "AND"
50 PRINT INT(6 * RND) + 1
60 END

RUN

GIVE ME A STARTING VALUE? 45
DICE TOSS
1
AND
3
```

Each time the program runs, the computer will use N to start the sequence of random numbers. Different values of N will produce different sequences.

If you wish any one number in a sequence of random numbers to be the same as the previous one, use RND(O).

```
10 INPUT "GIVE ME A STARTING VALUE"; N
20 PRINT "DICE TOSS"
30 PRINT INT(6 * RND(-N) ) + 1
40 PRINT "AND"
50 PRINT INT(6 * RND(O) ) + 1
60 END

RUN

GIVE ME A STARTING VALUE? 45
DICE TOSS
1
AND
1
```

The RANDOMIZE Statement

RANDOMIZE performs the same function as the negative argument of the RND function. It changes the computer's random number "seed" value. This program is equivalent to the dice toss program in Illustration 4.4:

```
10 INPUT "GIVE ME A STARTING VALUE"; N
20 RANDOMIZE N
30 PRINT "DICE TOSS"
40 PRINT INT(6 * RND) + 1
```

```
50 PRINT "AND"
60 PRINT INT(6 * RND) + 1
70 END

RUN

GIVE ME A STARTING VALUE? 33
DICE TOSS
5
AND
3
```

Different values of N will give different sequence of random numbers. If you do not enter a value for N, the computer will type:

```
RANDOM NUMBER SEED (-32768 TO 32767)?
```

and wait until you respond with a value in the range -32768 to 32767.

Large and Small Numbers

The computer uses floating-point, or exponential, notation in printing very large and small numbers. That is, it prints a number as a decimal with an exponent for the base number 10. This can easily be transcribed to the usual way of writing numbers, because the exponent tells you how many times to divide or multiply the given decimal by 10. If it is negative, divide by moving the decimal to the left. If it is positive, multiply by moving it to the right. Thus 1.234E-05 is .00001234, whereas 1.234E 05 is 123400.

In using the exponential notation, the computer gives you as many significant digits as it can print and still print the exponent. This may mean a loss of accuracy that you should be aware of. A number such as 345111002.1 might be printed as .345111E 09. You would have to interpret this as 345111000 and be only approximately correct. If you are concerned about accuracy, Chapter 12 explains how you can specify that numbers be stored with double precision of up to 16 (decimal) rather than the usual 7 digits of accuracy. The computer uses the floating-point format with a D in place of the E for printing a double precision number with many digits.

When you enter a number into the computer, you may use exponential notation to write very large or very small numbers. Or you may write out all of the digits. In either case, be sure not to use commas, because BASIC considers them as special characters that separate items. Write 1,456,878 as 1456878.

Problems

Order of Operations

1. Translate each of the following BASIC expressions into usual arithmetic expressions:

   a. (4^2*2^3)^.5

   b. 22/2*4 + 11-3^2/.3

   c. (.3/.9*3-9)^1/3

   d. 4 + 2/5-8 + 4^2

   e. (3*(4-2^4))^2

   f. 2 + 8/4-8*3^2

2. Write BASIC statements that make the following calculations and print out the results:

   a. $\dfrac{2 + 4^2}{5 \times 8}$

   b. $\dfrac{3 + 9}{8} - \dfrac{4 \times 2}{2^2}$

   c. $\dfrac{3(6.2 + 5)}{4.5 - 2.3}$

d. $10 \times \sqrt{25 + 11}$

e. $3.14R^2$

f. $2W + 9L$

g. $\left(\dfrac{3 + 12}{Y}\right)^2$

h. $\dfrac{1}{3 + \dfrac{1}{3 - \dfrac{1}{3 + 1}}}$

Corrections

3. In the space on the right, write "Correct" if the following BASIC statements are correctly entered. If not, rewrite them correctly. Consider each statement separately. These statements are not part of the same program.

   a. 30 PRINT A = 5*3/2 _____

   b. 33 PRINT "THE ANSWER IS": INT(X+ .5) _____

   c. 12 PRINT (3*X) + 4Y +Z^2 _____

   d. 37 PRINT X = C; X^2 = A; X^3 = B _____

   e. 17 PRINT SQR(84) _____

   f. 100 PRINT INT 150.75 _____

   g. 23 PRINT W, "FRED", T$, "TOM" _____

   h. 60 RANDOM _____

   i. 67 RANDOM X _____

   j. 90 R = RND _____

4. In the spaces on the right, write "Correct" if the following BASIC statements are correct. If not, rewrite them correctly. Consider each statement separately. These statements are not part of the same program.

   a. 45 PRINT RND _____

   b. 60 LET 2+4 = A _____

   c. 22 LET 3+7 _____

d. 10 LET A+B = 6 _____

e. 32 LET A = (S+X+Y)/3 _____

f. 24 C = SQR 25 _____

g. 55 P = P+2 _____

h. 34 F = F−7 _____

i. 65 P = P*N _____

j. 40 LET D = INT(10*RND+3) _____

5. Write a program that asks for a decimal number. Have the computer round it to the nearest integer and print out the result with a label explaining what it has done.

6. Write a program that prints the following table on the terminal after it is RUN:

Number	Square
2	4
3	9
4	16
5	25

7. Swifty Spritz is training for the Olympics as a freestyle swimmer. She swims 3 hours before breakfast and 2 1/2 hours each evening during the week. On Saturdays, she swims for 6 hours and on Sundays she takes a complete rest. Every minute she swims 4 lengths in the 25-yard pool, and each half-hour she burns 250 calories.

   Use the computer to determine how many calories she must add to her weekly diet in order not to lose weight during this period in her life. Also, calculate how many miles she swims each week.

8. Virtuous Vendor runs the bookstore but doesn't like to be bothered with change. All coins go to charity. Write a program that asks for the price of an item sold, prints out dollar amounts for Mr. Vendor and the change amount for charity, and then waits for the next transaction.

9. The Internal Revenue Service is very generous with taxpayers. If the tax you owe includes some change under 50¢, you need not send in the pennies. If the tax includes some change over 50¢, you are supposed to round up and send in the next highest dollar amount. Use the computer to let the taxpayer enter the exact amount of the

tax owed and have a printout of how much should be sent to Uncle Sam.

10. Use the computer to express your age in terms of years, months, and days. Assume that the average month has 30.4167 days.

11. The state lottery has tickets for the Juvenile, Adult, and Senior divisions. The ticket numbers for each division are in the following ranges:

Juvenile	1	to	100
Adult	101	to	200
Senior	201	to	250

    Use the computer to randomly select the winning ticket in each division.

12. Use the computer to determine how long a ladder is needed to rescue Purrky, the kitty, from the top of a 20-foot tree. Keep in mind that the foot of the ladder must be set 7 feet away from the base of the tree in order not to destroy the flower beds.

13. Mr. Jones and Mr. Smith each decided to buy one of the sailboats that were recently marked down from $1100 to $1000 for the Labor Day sale. Mr. Jones borrowed the purchase price and agreed to pay it back in one year with 14% interest. Mr. Smith decided not to borrow money but to save his pennies each month and purchase the boat outright at the end of the year. In so doing he lost the advantage of the sale price and was victimized by inflation that raised the regular price of the boat by 10%.

    Use the computer to determine how much more Mr. Smith paid for his sailboat. Express the difference as the amount as well as the percentage increase over Mr. Jones's expense.

Chapter 5

Cornerstones of Automation

Computers are automatons that do whatever they're told, whenever they're told, for however long they're told to work. In this they far surpass human beings. They don't take coffee breaks or holidays or even naps. They never get angry or fall in love, so they can give total attention to the most tedious and repetitious of chores.

But they are as dumb as they are diligent. If you set them in operation and never tell them to stop, they won't stop. This ability to proceed automatically is, indeed, another fundamental reason for the existence of computers as we know them; however, it must be channeled to produce meaningful solutions to real problems.

The BASIC language, like all computer languages, has several statements whose functions are to translate into appropriate computer actions the logic, or method, of solving a problem. These statements enable a computer to vary from its usual pattern of working its way line by line through a program from the first instruction to the last. They change the direction of control according to certain preset or even spontaneously created conditions. In some sense, they enable the computer to make decisions, and today computers automatically perform very sophisticated tasks. The challenge, of course, is to "fine-tune" these abilities and develop a true thinking machine.

This chapter presents the cornerstones of automation in BASIC: the GO TO, IF . . . THEN, and FOR . . . NEXT statements. There are fancier versions of these statements which you may want to use later on. But fancier is not always better, and you will be surprised by how much you can achieve with them in their most straightforward form.

The GO TO Statement

GO TO is the most primitive of the statements that provide automated logic, but it can keep your computer busy for a long time (Illustration 5.1).

ILLUSTRATION 5.1

GO TO always changes the direction of program control.

```
10 LET X = 0
20 LET X = X+1
30 PRINT X
40 GO TO 20
50 END
```

Now, take a minute to look at this program before setting it to run! It is the counting routine discussed in Chapter 3. If your computer were capable of handling all of the digits, it would begin with 1 and print successive whole numbers forever. Even a small computer will go up to a million and beyond. This is because the GO TO statement in line 40 changes the normal direction of the computer program. It sends the computer back to line 20, where X increases by 1. After line 30 prints the next X, program control reverses once again. The program is an infinite loop because the computer never reaches the END statement.

An endless loop is usually, but not always, a mistake. Once one is running, it can be intercepted by entering the CTRL/BREAK combination. Press the CTRL key, hold it down, and then press the BREAK key so that they are both down at once. Eventually the computer program will halt.

Now let the illustrated program run. Before you intervene, take a few seconds to marvel at the capacity of the computer to work quickly and repetitiously without making a mistake.

The GO TO statement is often described as an unconditional branch because it always sends control to another part of a program, either forward toward the END or backward. In doing so, it need not create a repetitive loop. It may simply branch to another program segment or to an exit point.

The IF . . . THEN Statement

Like a GO TO statement, IF . . . THEN changes the direction of program control. However, it does so only under certain conditions; see Illustration 5.2.

ILLUSTRATION 5.2

IF . . . THEN sets conditions for changing the direction of program control.

```
10 PRINT "ENTER YOUR AGE"
20 INPUT A
30 IF A=12 THEN GO TO 60
40 PRINT "SORRY, FIND ANOTHER TEAM."
50 GO TO 70
60 PRINT "YOU MAY PLAY WITH US."
70 END

RUN

ENTER YOUR AGE
?10
SORRY, FIND ANOTHER TEAM.

RUN

ENTER YOUR AGE
?12
YOU MAY PLAY WITH US.
```

Line 30 asks whether the value input for A is 12. If it is, control passes to line 60. If A is not 12, control passes in the usual manner to the next line of the program, line 40.

This example of conditional branching enables the computer to rather roughly evaluate the information entered; it distinguishes between an age of 12 and all other ages. The programmer has used this to have the computer print appropriate responses as the program runs. Only 12-year-olds are encouraged to play on our team.

There are several relations that IF . . . THEN can evaluate. The relations and their symbols are:

=	Equal to
>	Greater than
<	Less than
>=	Greater than or equal to
<=	Less than or equal to
<>	Not equal to

These permit more precise analysis, as in Illustration 5.3. Here, IF . . . THEN asks whether A is greater than or equal to 18, the legal voting age. Control passes to line 60 only if a value that satisfies either of the conditions is entered for A. When A is less than 18, the computer continues to the next line.

ILLUSTRATION 5.3

IF . . . THEN checks relations (greater than or equal to).

```
10 PRINT "ENTER YOUR AGE"
20 INPUT A
30 IF A >= 18 THEN GO TO 60
40 PRINT "YOU ARE TOO YOUNG"
50 GO TO 70
60 PRINT "YOU MAY VOTE."
70 END
```

Notice that you don't have to write another IF . . . THEN to check for A < 18 (less than) in line 40. This is because you know how IF . . . THEN works in line 30, and you know that if control reaches line 40, the computer has proved that A is less than 18. You can go ahead and print the response you want to give people who are too young to vote. In general, use one less IF . . . THEN than the number of possible relations.

Once you are familiar with IF . . . THEN, take advantage of the shortcuts you are allowed. Delete the GO TO after THEN and simply specify the line number that is your destination. The following two lines are equivalent:

```
10 IF I = 33 THEN 100
10 IF I = 33 THEN GO TO 100
```

Or, delete the word THEN and just use GO TO:

```
10 IF I = 33 GO TO 100
```

The relational comparisons made by IF . . . THEN can be quite fancy. Variables can be compared to one another. Expressions can be evaluated and then compared. All of the following statements are good IF . . . THENs:

```
10 IF A + B < 16 THEN 100
10 IF A ^ 2 = C THEN 100
10 IF 16 ^ 3 = C/3 THEN 100
10 IF A >= B THEN 100
```

String Comparisons with IF . . . THEN

Conditional branching with character string data brings the power of the computer to innumerable areas of human endeavor. Not only numbers but also facts, feelings, and opinions can be evaluated and used to direct the computer. The relational symbols and their meaning for character data are:

=   Equal to (identical, no leading or trailing blanks)
<   Less than (closer to the beginning of the alphabet, shorter)
>   Greater than (closer to the end of the alphabet, longer)

Illustration 5.4 sends ticket holders to their seats. The theater manager has decided that all those whose names precede M in the alphabet must sit in the balcony. The other patrons may sit in the orchestra. Line 20 asks whether the data stored in N$ is alphabetically closer to Z than the character M. When Paula, which is nearer to Z, is entered as N$, control passes to line 50. When Betty is entered, however, the greater-than comparison (>) does not hold. Betty is less than M, so control falls to line 30. N$ = "M" is not considered because a name consisting only of M is not a possibility.

ILLUSTRATIONS 5.4

IF . . . THEN makes alphabetical comparisons of character data.

```
10 INPUT "ENTER YOUR NAME" ;N$
20 IF N$>"M" THEN 50
30 PRINT "SIT IN THE BALCONY"
40 GO TO 60
50 PRINT "SIT IN THE ORCHESTRA"
60 END
```

```
RUN

ENTER YOUR NAME? PAULA
SIT IN THE ORCHESTRA

RUN

ENTER YOUR NAME? BETTY
SIT IN THE BALCONY
```

The computer is actually making numerical comparisons when it processes character data in relational expressions. It compares the computer's numeric equivalents for the characters and branches accordingly.

One great advantage of using character data is that it helps to personalize computing and make people feel at home. But you must proceed somewhat cautiously, because programs that manipulate string data are dealing with two very different creatures. Humans are capricious; computers are never capricious. For example, a programmer might type the M in line 20 of Illustration 5.4 as "M", or as " M", or "M ", with leading or trailing spaces. If the value entered for N$ happened to be M alone, the computer would compare line 20 with the character M, making no allowances for the programmer's errors in spacing. It would consider:

1. (space) M to be less than M
2. M (space) to be greater than M

In the first instance, a blank character, or blank space, has a lower numeric equivalent than M. In the second instance, the null character appended to M makes it a longer character string than M alone. If all other things are equal, a longer string is greater than a shorter one.

Chapter 8 discusses the character string functions that help to check for and accommodate these human inconsistencies. You will see that with meticulous programming you can create appropriate computer responses. But the ability to completely blend computer and human responses is the continuing goal of artificial intelligence research.

AND and OR with IF . . . THEN

AND and OR are logical operators that are used frequently in IF
. . . THEN statements to compare two or more relations:

```
10 IF X = 12 AND Y < 0 THEN 100
```

sends control to line 100 if both X = 12 and Y < 0 are true. The
statement:

```
10 IF X = 12 OR Y < 0 THEN 100
```

sends control to line 100 when either X = 12 or Y < 0 is true.

Complex IF . . . THEN

BASIC allows you to append statements other than GO TO to
the THEN. You can write:

```
25 IF X = 6 THEN PRINT "HI MAMA!"
20 IF X = 6 THEN LET A = 54

15 IF X$ = "NO" THEN IF Y$ = "MAYBE" THEN PRINT
"SORRY"
99 IF X$ = "NO" THEN INPUT Y$
```

Remember when you use these constructions that the line following
your fancy IF . . . THEN will also be executed. There is no longer
a branch. If the comparison is true, the additional BASIC statement
is executed and then control continues sequentially through the
program statements. If the comparison is false, the additional statement is ignored (Illustration 5.5).

ILLUSTRATION 5.5

Appending PRINT to IF . . . THEN

```
10 PRINT "ENTER THE MONTH"
20 INPUT M$
30 IF M$ = "MAY" THEN PRINT "SPRING IS HERE!"
40 PRINT "I LOVE SPRINGTIME!"
50 END

RUN
```

```
ENTER THE MONTH
? JANUARY
I LOVE SPRINGTIME!

RUN

ENTER THE MONTH
? MAY
SPRING IS HERE!
I LOVE SPRINGTIME!
```

The ability to append complicated BASIC statements to IF . . . THEN is both a blessing and a curse. Good programming requires that program instructions be easy to read and to test for errors. Statements that solve complex problems in one line are likely to be difficult to decipher. If they are, they will limit your program's usefulness. As you work, keep in mind the importance of a good balance between efficiency and clarity.

IF . . . THEN . . . ELSE

ELSE provides an alternative to the THEN clause in an IF . . . THEN statement by specifying what to do when the relation is false. ELSE is powerful because when it is appended, a single IF statement tells the computer how to handle both TRUE and FALSE conditions:

```
10 IF X = 45 THEN 50 ELSE PRINT "WRONG"
```

If X = 45 is not the case, the message WRONG is printed. When X = 45 is true, control is sent to line 50.

ILLUSTRATION 5.6

Simple IF . . . THEN

```
10  X = 0
20  X = X+1
30  PRINT "WAKE UP!!"
40  IF X = 3 THEN 60
50  GO TO 20
60  END


RUN


WAKE UP!!
WAKE UP!!
WAKE UP!!
```

ILLUSTRATION 5.7

Complex IF . . . THEN

```
10 X = 0
20 X = X+1
30 IF X = 4 THEN 50 ELSE PRINT "WAKE UP!!"
40 GO TO 20
50 END


RUN


WAKE UP!!
WAKE UP!!
WAKE UP!!
```

ELSE produces complicated statements. Use it carefully. Compare the programs of Illustrations 5.6 and 5.7. They both use IF . . . THEN to stop the computer after it prints WAKE UP!! three times. Illustration 5.7 is shorter because the ELSE clause includes the PRINT statement, but its logic is harder to follow. Illustration 5.6 is a better illustration of good programming style.

FOR . . . NEXT Statements

The FOR . . . NEXT combination of statements creates and controls program loops. Unlike Illustration 5.1, which would have gone on counting forever, Illustration 5.8 counts up to 3 and no more. This is because FOR and NEXT provide an exit mechanism for the loop.

FOR is actually a fancy LET statement that stores the beginning and ending values for a counter as well as all of the values in between. In the FOR . . . NEXT example in Illustration 5.8, X is the counter that starts as 1 and progresses by 1's up to 3.

NEXT is a fancy GO TO statement that increments the counting variable and determines if it has exceeded the ending limit. If it has, there is no looping back. If it has not, the loop repeats for another turn. In Illustration 5.8, the NEXT statement repeatedly increments X and compares its value to 3, the limit set in line 10. When X exceeds that limit, control is sent forward to the next line of the program, line 40. The value of X is printed exactly three times, no more, no less.

ILLUSTRATION 5.8

FOR . . . NEXT creates and controls program loops.

```
10 FOR X = 1 TO 3
20     PRINT X
30 NEXT X
40 END

RUN

   1
   2
   3
```

The job within the loop may be quite long and complicated. It may be a whole program or a small detail in a large project. It may even be instructions to execute another loop. Regardless, the computer will repeat the instructions of the lines that fall between FOR and NEXT however many times are specified at the start. Illustration 5.9 sends junk mail to four people. Notice that the lines within the loop have been indented by 5 spaces. The computer doesn't require this, but writing FOR . . . NEXT loops according to this convention makes your programs a lot easier for humans to understand.

ILLUSTRATION 5.9

FOR . . . NEXT controls the number of letters to be printed.

```
10 FOR X = 1 TO 4
20     READ N$
30     PRINT "DEAR "; N$
40     PRINT
50     PRINT "PLEASE VISIT OUR NEW STORE"
60     PRINT "AND PICK UP A FREE PRIZE"
70     PRINT
80 NEXT X
90 DATA MR. ADAMS, MRS. BAKER
100 DATA MR. CHARLIE, MR. DOE
110 END

RUN

DEAR MR. ADAMS

PLEASE VISIT OUR NEW STORE
AND PICK UP A FREE PRIZE

DEAR MRS. BAKER

PLEASE VISIT OUR NEW STORE
AND PICK UP A FREE PRIZE

DEAR MR. CHARLIE

PLEASE VISIT OUR NEW STORE
AND PICK UP A FREE PRIZE

DEAR MR. DOE

PLEASE VISIT OUR NEW STORE
AND PICK UP A FREE PRIZE
```

Each time the loop repeats, the READ in line 20 stores a new name and moves the arrow to the next one in DATA. The program works because there is a match between the number of times the loop will execute and the number of names. We could produce 15 letters by adding 11 more names and changing line 10 to:

```
10 FOR X = 1 TO 15
```

The counting variable has many more uses than just storing the incremental values of the loop. It is useful within the loop as well (Illustration 5.10). You know that lines 20 and 40 together guarantee a succession of X values from 1 to 5, so you can use a FOR . . . NEXT loop to produce a table of the squares and the cubes of those numbers.

ILLUSTRATION 5.10

Using the FOR . . . NEXT control variable within the loop

```
10 PRINT "NO.", "SQUARE", "CUBE"
20 FOR X = 1 TO 5
30     PRINT X, X ^ 2, X ^ 3
40 NEXT X
50 END

RUN
```

NO.	SQUARE	CUBE
1	1	1
2	4	8
3	9	27
4	16	64
5	25	125

In fact, you can use this loop to do any job that requires such a succession of values. In Illustration 5.11, the computer uses the counter to print out the position of a name in a list as well as the name itself.

ILLUSTRATION 5.11

Using the FOR . . . NEXT control variable within the loop

```
10 FOR X = 1 TO 5
20 READ N$
30     PRINT X;" ";N$
40 NEXT X
50 DATA KEN, LOU, HAL, NED, ORV
60 END

RUN
```

```
1 KEN
2 LOU
3 HAL
4 NED
5 ORV
```

Using the counter within the loop is clearly very handy. But you must be careful not to *change* the counter within the loop. This must be done by the NEXT statement only, or the loop will not follow the plan set out in the FOR statement. In Illustration 5.12 a LET statement included by mistake drastically changes the outcome of the program.

ILLUSTRATION 5.12

Mistakenly changing the FOR . . . NEXT control variable within the loop

```
10 FOR X = 1 TO 5
20     LET X = 900
30     READ N$
40     PRINT X;" ";N$
50 NEXT X
60 DATA KEN, LOU, HAL, NED, ORV
70 END

RUN

 900  KEN
```

By the time control reaches the NEXT statement, X has been changed to 900, far beyond the limit of 5 set forth in line 10. So the computer, which never questions the wisdom of an instruction, terminates the loop.

The counter need not always start at 1 and go up by 1's to whatever limit is set. It can start anywhere and go up by any increment that is useful to the problem at hand. To create a table of the squares of all of the even numbers from 1 to 10, write Illustration 5.13.

ILLUSTRATION 5.13

STEP sets the increment for the FOR . . . NEXT control variable.

```
10 FOR X = 2 TO 10 STEP 2
20     PRINT X,X↑2
30 NEXT X
40 END
```

RUN

2	4
4	16
6	36
8	64
10	100

The STEP modifier in line 10 tells the computer to add 2 to the counting variable after each iteration. The computer will keep looping back until this size increment makes the counter greater than the limit. Thus, in Illustration 5.13, X is 2, 4, 6, 8, and 10, while looping occurs. When X reaches 12, control is sent to line 40.

Variables and arithmetic expressions can be used throughout the right side of the FOR statement. You don't have to know what the beginning, ending, or step values of the counter will be when you write your program. They can be entered when the program runs. Try running the previous illustration using some of the FOR statements below.

```
10 FOR X = 100 TO 1000 STEP 2

10 FOR X = A TO B STEP 5 (Use INPUT to define the
                          values for A and B
                          before line 10.)

10 FOR X = A/2 TO 50 STEP 2

10 FOR X = 16 TO 32 STEP 5

10 FOR X = 16 TO 32 STEP A

10 FOR X = 100 TO 1 STEP -1 (You can even count
                             down.)
```

Notice how frequently the STEP modifier is used. The only time you don't need it is when you want to count up by ones.

Nested FOR . . . NEXT Statements

It is often very useful to have one loop occur within another loop. If you wanted to print out the list of names in Illustration 5.11 two times, Illustration 5.14 shows what you would do.

ILLUSTRATION 5.14

Nesting FOR . . . NEXT loops like paper cups in a stack

```
10 FOR Y = 1 TO 2
15     PRINT "THIS IS LIST NO.";Y
20     FOR X = 1 TO 5
30         READ N$
35         PRINT N$
40     NEXT X
45     PRINT
46     RESTORE
50 NEXT Y
60 DATA KEN,LOU,HAL,NED,ORV
70 END

RUN

THIS IS LIST NO. 1
KEN
LOU
HAL
NED
ORV

THIS IS LIST NO. 2
KEN
LOU
HAL
NED
ORV
```

This technique is known as nesting, and quite properly so. It has the important requirement that the inner loop must be completely nested within the outer loop. That is, the inner loop must run to completion during a single iteration of the outer loop. Here, the entire list of names is printed by the X loop before the RESTORE statement executes and the Y counter goes up in line 50.

When they are properly nested, all of the loops have the chance to run completely. If they are meshed in any other way, one will invariably be interrupted and even the normally quite obedient computer will complain. In Illustration 5.15, the loop combination reverses the NEXT statements. It may seem to make sense, but the program won't work because the second loop never gets a chance to run completely.

ILLUSTRATION 5.15

Improper nesting of FOR . . . NEXT loops

```
10 FOR Y = 1 TO 2
20     FOR X = 1 TO 10
30          READ N$
35          PRINT N$
40     NEXT Y
50     PRINT
55     RESTORE
60 NEXT X
70 DATA KEN,LOU,HAL,NED,ORV,PAT,RON,SID,TED,UNC
80 END

RUN

NEXT WITHOUT FOR
```

Have as many loops within one another as your computer will hold. But be sure to nest them like paper cups in a stack, one inside another.

NEXT Variations

You can write a line like

```
210 NEXT
```

with no variable and this will speed up the execution of the FOR . . . NEXT loop. You can also combine NEXT statements if they would otherwise come one after the other. Write:

```
210 NEXT X, Y
```

rather than

```
200 NEXT X
210 NEXT Y
```

These shortcuts are good ones as long as they do not make the structure of your program hard to follow.

Reminders for using FOR . . . NEXT

1. Use the counter within the loop if you wish. But be sure not to change it by any means other than the NEXT statement.
2. The counting variable can step up or down. If you wish it

changed in a way other than up by 1 each time, you must use the STEP modifier.

3. It is correct to leave a loop in the middle by a branching statement such as IF . . . THEN or GO TO, and you can even leave the loop and come back to the middle. But you should never enter a loop for the first time in the middle. Start with the FOR statement.

4. A loop within a loop must be completely nested. The FOR and the NEXT of the inner loop occur between the FOR and NEXT of the outer loop.

The WHILE and WEND Statements

These statements combine features of both the IF . . . THEN and FOR . . . NEXT statements. Like IF . . . THEN, they allow you to make a comparison and then branch according to the results. Like FOR . . . NEXT, they create a program loop.

The WHILE statement precedes the program statements that comprise the body of the loop and sets up the conditions that activate the loop. The WEND statement, like the NEXT statement, forms the final line of the program loop. Each time control reaches WEND, the computer checks to see if the criteria set up in the WHILE statement have been met. If not, control falls to the line following the WEND statement. If so, passage through the loop occurs another time. Illustration 5.16 uses WHILE and WEND to force a user to enter the secret password before RUNning the rest of the program.

ILLUSTRATION 5.16

Using WHILE and WEND

```
10 WHILE PAS$ <> "PETUNIA"
20    INPUT""ENTER THE PASSWORD"; PAS$
30 WEND
40 PRINT "WELCOME ABOARD"
50 END

RUN

ENTER THE PASSWORD? ICICLE
ENTER THE PASSWORD? FINCHES
ENTER THE PASSWORD? PETUNIA
WELCOME ABOARD
```

Problems

Corrections

1. In the spaces on the right, write ''Correct'' if the following BASIC statements are correct. If not, rewrite them correctly. Consider each statement separately. These statements are not part of the same program.

   a. 88 GO TO X _____

   b. 55 GO TO END _____

   c. 67 GO TO LINE 200 _____

   d. 70 FOR X = A TO B STEP C _____

   e. 65 IF Y = 76 THEN PRINT "CRACKERS" _____

   f. 85 IF W = 100 THEN Z = Z+1 _____

   g. 80 FOR X = 1 – 5 _____

   h. 35 IF S = 9 THEN 36 _____

   i. 69 NEXT X, Y _____

   j. 20 FOR X = 1 TO 10 WHILE A < 5 _____

2. In the spaces on the right, write ''Correct'' if the following BASIC statements are correct. If not, rewrite them correctly. Consider each statement separately. These statements are not part of the same program.

   a. 75 FOR T = 4 TO 12 STEP 2 _____

   b. 2 IF G = T AND H = T THEN 45 _____

   c. 50 STEP 5 _____

   d. 25 NEXT 10 _____

   e. 78 FOR Y = 112 TO 56 STEP –12 _____

f. 45 NEXT X _____

g. 86 NEXT STEP _____

h. 70 IF X+Y > 57 THEN 100 _____

i. 20 IF Y = 38 THEN 16 _____

j. 15 LET X + 1 TO 25 STEP 5 _____

3. In the spaces on the right, write "Correct" if the following BASIC statements are correct. If not, rewrite them correctly. Consider each statement separately. These statements are not part of the same program.

a. 67 NEXT X^2 _____

b. 12 IF X + Y = B THEN 150 _____

c. 10 FOR G = 100 TO 0 STEP B _____

d. 8 NEXT _____

e. 56 IF A = B THEN GO TO LINE 120 _____

f. 71 IF INT X = 2 THEN 55 _____

g. 30 FOR 4*B TO C STEP −5 _____

h. 8 IF " END" > N$ THEN PRINT "FINISHED" _____

i. 75 IF N$ = "MARY" THEN 42 _____

j. 22 IF K$ < "PIZZA" THEN 100 _____

4. In the spaces on the right, write "Correct" if the following BASIC statements are correct. If not, rewrite them correctly. Consider the statements separately. These statements are not part of the same program.

a. 30 FOR P$ = 100 TO 1 STEP −2 _____

b. 70 IF A$ = HUNTINGTON THEN 80 _____

c. 8 IF A\$ = B\$ THEN 100 _____

d. 25 IF "YOUR NAME" > "MY NAME" THEN 60 _____

e. 22 IF A\$ = "YES" THEN END _____

f. 60 IF G\$ = 234 THEN 100 _____

g. 65 IF "EASTER" = A\$ THEN GO TO 80 _____

h. WEND X _____

i. WHILE A\$ = "SECRET" _____

j. WEND F = 45 _____

Programs to read

In the space on the right, write what will be printed when the following programs are run. If input from the terminal is needed, show some sample input that would fit with the program.

```
5. 10 INPUT F
   20 FOR X = 1 TO F
   30     PRINT "THUNDER"
   40     PRINT
   50 NEXT X
   60 IF X = F THEN 80
   70 PRINT "SUNSHINE"
   80 PRINT "LIGHTNING"
   90 END

6. 10 LET Y = 31.4
   20 IF INT(Y) = Y THEN 55
   30 PRINT "HALLOWEEN"
   40 LET Y = Y/2 -5.7
   50 GO TO 20
   55 PRINT "PUMPKINS"
   60 LET P = Y+1
   70 IF P <> 10 THEN 100
   80 GO TO 20
   100 END

7. 10 FOR X = 3 TO 19 STEP 4
   20     PRINT X-2
```

```
   30      PRINT X+2
   40 NEXT X
   50 END

8. 10 DATA 5,15,10
   20 READ R,S
   30 PRINT R+S
   40 READ T
   50 RESTORE
   60 READ U,V,W
   70 IF T = U THEN 100
   80 IF S = V THEN 110
   90 GO TO 120
   100 PRINT "WRONG"
   105 GO TO 120
   110 PRINT "RIGHT"
   120 END

9. 10 PRINT "STAND BY FOR AIR TIME"
   20 FOR K = 5 TO 1 STEP -1
   30 PRINT K;" SECONDS"
   40 GO TO 10
   50 PRINT "YOU'RE ON!"
   60 END

10. 10 LET A = 10
    20 LET B = 10
    30 LET K = 1
    40 IF K >= 5 THEN 100
    50 PRINT K,A,B
    60 LET A = A+2
    70 LET B = A+B
    80 LET K = K+1
    90 GO TO 40
    100 END

11. 10 FOR N = 0 TO 50 STEP 5
    20      T = T+N*2
    30 NEXT N
    40 PRINT N
    45 END

12. 10 FOR P = 8 TO 30 STEP 6
    20      PRINT "HELLO"
    30 NEXT P
    40 PRINT "GOODBYE"
    50 END
```

13. ```
    10 H = 1
    20 PRINT H
    30 LET H = H+1
    40 IF H <= 10 THEN 20
    50 END
    ```

14. ```
    10 FOR I = 1 TO 2
    20     FOR J = 1 TO 4
    30           PRINT I,J
    40     NEXT J
    50 NEXT I
    60 END
    ```

15. ```
    10 FOR X = 2 TO 4
    20     PRINT X,X*X
    30 NEXT X
    40 END
    ```

16. ```
    10 FOR K = 1 TO 3
    20     LET P = 2^K
    30     PRINT K,P
    40 NEXT K
    50 END
    ```

17. ```
    10 FOR X = 1 TO 10
    20 PRINT X,X^2
    30 STEP 2
    40 PRINT "ALL FINISHED!"
    50 END
    ```

18. ```
    10 FOR L = 1 TO 5
    20     FOR S = 1 TO L
    30           PRINT "1 ";
    50           NEXT S
    60 PRINT
    70 NEXT L
    80 END
    ```

19. ```
    10 LET A = 5
    20 LET B = 78
    30 LET C = 45
    40 FOR T = 100 TO 1 STEP -1
    50     IF T = A THEN PRINT T,
    60     IF T = B THEN PRINT T,
    70     IF T = C THEN PRINT T,
    80 NEXT T
    90 END
    ```
    ```

20.
```
10  PRINT "TYPE IN YOUR NAME"
20  INPUT N$
30  IF "CHRISTMAS" < "HALLOWEEN" THEN 60
40  PRINT "TRICK OR TREAT"
50  GO TO 100
60  PRINT "HO! HO! HO!"
100 END
```

21.
```
10  READ A$,B$
20  IF A$ = "-1" THEN PRINT "THAT'S ALL FOLKS"
30  RESTORE
40  READ Q$
50  IF Q$ = "-1" THEN 40
60  PRINT Q$
70  DATA "THE DUCK FAMILY"
80  DATA -1, HUEY, LOOEY, DUEY
90  END
```

22.
```
10  LET P = 4
20  FOR L = 1 TO 6
30      LET X = RND(0)
40      IF X < 5 THEN 130
50      P = P+.5
60      GO TO 140
130     P = P-.5
140 NEXT L
150 PRINT P
999 END
```

23.
```
10  WHILE X < 100
20        PRINT X
30  WEND
40  END
```

24.
```
10  WHILE C$ <> "HIST"
20        READ C$, E$
30        PRINT "COURSE ";C$
40        PRINT "ENROLLMENT ";E$
50  WEND
60  DATA MATH, 23, ENG, 20, HIST, 18, ART, 20
```

Programs to write

25. To attract new business the snack bar is offering sodas at a nickel per can with a limit of six per customer. Write a program that monitors the quantity sold each time and prints a warning if a customer tries to buy too many.

26. Have the computer ask a person's age. Then print out YOU ARE A SUPERSTAR once for every year of his life.

27. Write a computer program that asks a person for her age. If she is 18 or over, tell her she is old enough to vote. Otherwise, tell her how long she must wait.

28. Write a program that quizzes the user on the 9 times tables. When the quiz is finished, tell her how many she got correct.

29. Write a computer program that stores in a DATA statement the current registration figures for the adult education classes. Ask a potential student the number of the course he wants to take and tell him if there is any room left for him. Each course is limited to an enrollment of 20.

30. Each Tuesday the participants in Wait Watchers line up in their usual order and weigh in. Write a program that keeps track of all 15 dieters' last week's weight. As they enter this week's poundage, have the computer print CONGRATULATIONS! if they have lost weight. Otherwise tell them how much they gained.

31. Write a program that asks the U.S. Olympic cross-country skiing coach for the time in minutes and seconds of the gold, silver, and bronze medalists in the 30-kilometer event. If anyone was less than a second faster than the next slowest time, have the computer print THIS WAS REALLY A TIE FOR THE ——————— MEDAL.

32. Write a program that acts like an adding machine. Every time a number is entered, it is added to the previous numbers. When all of the numbers have been entered, the sum is printed.

33. Write a computer program that keeps track of the supply of mint chocolate chip and chocolate ice cream and watermelon sherbet for the Tutti Frutti Ice Cream Parlor. When a cone is sold, subtract that amount (1 cone = 4 ounces). If the supply of any one gets down to 1 gallon, have the computer tell the manager which flavor must be replenished.

34. Write a computer quiz on any topic you choose. Give the contestant five questions and a cheery response if the answer is correct. Give a sad reply if the answer is wrong. Keep score and print out the results.

35. Use WHILE and WEND to control a loop that reads DATA containing states and their capitals. Quiz the user about the capital of each state and tell him whether his answer is right or wrong. End the program when all of the questions have been asked.

Part Three

Commonly Used Features

Chapter 6

Subscripted Variables

Let's keep a list of the birds we've seen on our morning jogs. They are so plentiful that we ought to store them in a DATA statement and call them up with READ.

ILLUSTRATION 6.1

Ordinary variables are useful for small amounts of data but inadequate for long lists.

```
10 PRINT "THE BEAUTIFUL BIRDS WE'VE SEEN ARE:"
20 PRINT
30 READ A$, B$, C$, D$, E$
40 PRINT "MONDAY ", A$
50 PRINT "TUESDAY ", B$
60 PRINT "WEDNESDAY ", C$
70 PRINT "THURSDAY ", D$
80 PRINT "FRIDAY ", E$
90 DATA REDHEADED WOODPECKER, SCARLET TANAGER
100 DATA CARDINAL, BOBOLINK, GOLDFINCH
110 END

RUN

THE BEAUTIFUL BIRDS WE'VE SEEN ARE:

MONDAY       REDHEADED WOODPECKER
TUESDAY      SCARLET TANAGER
```

```
WEDNESDAY      CARDINAL
THURSDAY       BOBOLINK
FRIDAY         GOLDFINCH
```

If we go jogging more often, we're likely to have a very long list of birds and our READ and PRINT routine will soon become unwieldy. There will be too many variables to type, and we may even run out of allowable variables altogether. We are faced with the problem of how to efficiently store and retrieve lists of related information. Technically known as list processing (or array handling or matrix manipulation), this need is so common that BASIC and most computer languages have statements which make this job easy.

The DIMension Statement

In BASIC, the DIM statement informs the computer of the name and the length of the list (Illustration 6.2).

ILLUSTRATION 6.2

DIM sets the name and the number of subscripted variables.

```
10 DIM B$(5)
20 PRINT "THE BEAUTIFUL BIRDS WE'VE SEEN ARE:"
30 PRINT
40 READ B$(1), B$(2), B$(3), B$(4), B$(5)
50 PRINT "MONDAY ", B$(1)
60 PRINT "TUESDAY ", B$(2)
70 PRINT "WEDNESDAY ", B$(3)
80 PRINT "THURSDAY ", B$(4)
90 PRINT "FRIDAY ", B$(5)
100 DATA REDHEADED WOODPECKER, SCARLET TANAGER
100 DATA CARDINAL, BOBOLINK, GOLDFINCH
120 END

RUN

THE BEAUTIFUL BIRDS WE'VE SEEN ARE:

MONDAY         REDHEADED WOODPECKER
TUESDAY        SCARLET TANAGER
WEDNESDAY      CARDINAL
THURSDAY       BOBOLINK
FRIDAY         GOLDFINCH
```

Line 10 of Illustration 6.2 tells the computer to set aside six consecutive memory locations for the elements of the list B$. A subscript written as a number in parentheses denotes the relative position of each element and distinguishes one from the other. B$(0) is the first, B$(1) follows, and B$(5) is the sixth, or last, in the list. Once the list is dimensioned, the variables associated with it are known to the computer and you can use them like any other variables in your program. Line 40, the READ statement, assigns data to the variables of the list. Lines 50 through 90 reference the subscripted variables in order to print the list.

The OPTION BASE Statement

Programmers rarely use B$(0), the zero element. Usually, it is clearer to match the subscripts and the position of the data. In Illustration 6.2, B$(0) is ignored, and the first bird has subscript (1). The fifth is B$(5).

Because of this, IBM personal computer BASIC makes it possible to specify that the lowest subscript for any array in your program will be one (1). Enter the line:

```
10 OPTION BASE 1
```

before any DIM statements.

Using Arrays Effectively

Illustration 6.2 is not more efficient than 6.1. The power of subscripted variables emerges when you take advantage of the fact that *the subscript itself can be a variable*. By using a FOR . . . NEXT loop you can work with a list of 500 birds as easily as a list of 5 (Illustration 6.3).

ILLUSTRATION 6.3

Subscripts make processing long lists as easy as processing short ones.

```
10 DIM B$(500)              10 DIM C$(5)
20 FOR X = 1 TO 500         20 FOR X = 1 TO 5
30 READ B$(X)               30 READ C$(X)
40 PRINT "DAY"; X, B$(X)    40 PRINT "DAY"; X, C$(X)
50 NEXT X                   50 NEXT X
60 DATA BLUEBIRD, CANARY    60 DATA BLUEBIRD, CANARY
```

```
70 DATA CROW, PARROT, OWL        70 DATA CROW, PARROT, OWL
 . DATA ... 495 ...              80 END
 . DATA ... more ...
 . DATA ... birds ...            RUN
999 END
                                 DAY 1          BLUEBIRD
                                 DAY 2          CANARY
RUN                              DAY 3          CROW
                                 DAY 4          PARROT
DAY 1          BLUEBIRD          DAY 5          OWL
DAY 2          CANARY
DAY 3          CROW
DAY 4          PARROT
DAY 5          OWL

                 .
                 .
                 .
```

and on and on for 495 more birds

```
    .
    .
    .
```

    The same short READ and PRINT statements in lines 30 and 40 retrieve all of the data in both examples in the illustration. This is because they are embedded in FOR . . . NEXT loops and use the counting variable for a subscript. As X progresses from 1 to 5 or 500 with FOR . . . NEXT, so do the subscripts in lines 30 and 40. First B\$(1) and C\$(1) are read and printed, then B\$(2) and C\$(2) and so on until X passes the limit established in line 20.

    Variables as subscripts make many things possible. They are particularly useful for searching through and sorting out lists. If you decide to arrange your list of birds according to your sighting on each day of your week's vacation, you can easily recall which one you saw on a particular day (Illustration 6.4).

ILLUSTRATION 6.4

A variable as a subscript permits the direct access of any list item.

```
10 DIM B$(7)
20 FOR X = 1 TO 7
30 READ B$(X)
40 NEXT X
50 INPUT "WHICH DAY INTERESTS YOU"; D
60 PRINT "THE BIRD WE SAW ON DAY"; D; "WAS A:"
```

```
70 PRINT B$(D)
80 DATA BLACKBIRD, EAGLE, HAWK, SWAN
85 DATA OSTRICH, PEACOCK, PHEASANT
90 END

RUN

WHICH DAY INTERESTS YOU? 3
THE BIRD WE SAW ON DAY 3 WAS A:
HAWK

RUN

WHICH DAY INTERESTS YOU? 6
THE BIRD WE SAW ON DAY 6 WAS A:
PEACOCK
```

Line 10 in Illustration 6.4 reserves memory space for the list and establishes its variables. Lines 20 through 40 sequentially assign all of the data to the variables in the list. Because you carefully put the bird you saw on day 1 first in the data and also positioned the others according to the day they were seen, the subscripts match the vacation day that each bird was sighted.

When you inquire about a particular day through the INPUT statement in line 50, it is a simple matter to locate the correct bird. The day you are curious about, D, becomes the subscript, and the information stored in that position in the list is retrieved by the PRINT statement in line 70.

Not only can subscripts be variables, but they can also be expressions. It is correct to write:

```
10 PRINT X(C+6)
```

The computer calculates the value of C + 6 and retrieves data from that position in the list X.

DIM statements can accommodate more than one list at a time:

```
10 DIM A(50), A$(10), Z(100)
```

One list with space for 51 numbers (remember the zero element) called A, one for 11 character strings called A$, and another numeric list for 101 elements called Z are all reserved in memory.

BASIC allows arrays of 11 elements (0 through 10) to be used without being defined in a DIM statement. That is, mention of an array element as in LET A(5) = 6 implies the existence of the array A with elements A(0) through A(10). Or, if you had specified OPTION BASE 1 at the beginning of your program, the array would have elements A(1) through A(10).

The ERASE Statement

BASIC does not allow you to change the size of an array once it has been dimensioned. However, you can erase any number of arrays with the ERASE statement and then redefine them:

```
10 DIM BUG(160,100), BEE (200,20), BEETLE(30)
   .
   .
   .
50 ERASE BUG, BEETLE
   .
   .
75 DIM BUG(12)
```

Matrices: Arrays with Many Dimensions

BASIC allows you to have up to 255 dimensions for an array and up to 32767 elements per dimension! Think carefully before you take advantage of these capacities. If you make your arrays too large you may not only run out of computer space, but you may also have a hard time remembering how to access any one data item. Sometimes, however, multidimensional arrays (matrices), are the only solution to a problem.

Two-dimensional arrays are very frequently used. Often it is not helpful to relate information by a position in a list. How hard it would be to find a seat in the stadium if your ticket were stamped with a single number telling which of the many seats it represents! Tickets with two notations do a good job. They tell you where to sit by pinpointing first your row and then your seat.

The mapmakers of the world also use this convention. Paris, Oslo, and Rome are located not as 1, 2, or 300, but in terms of degrees of latitude and longitude: two numbers that tell how far they lie north or south of the equator and east or west of the prime meridian.

BASIC allows you to organize information in this way. As you plan your program you can conceive of a rectangular honeycomb, or matrix, in which to store your data. You can put each item in a "cell" and retrieve any one by referring to its row and column address. The DIM statement establishes the name and the dimension of the matrix:

```
10 DIM A(2,3)
```

This tells the computer to reserve two rows and three columns in memory for the numeric information that will be placed in matrix A. Actually, as shown in Illustration 6.5, the computer allows an additional zero row and zero column. A double subscript distinguishes each element. The first number gives the row address; the second gives the column address.

ILLUSTRATION 6.5

Matrix A in memory

	Column 0	Column 1	Column 2	Column 3
Row 0	0,0	0,1	0,2	0,3
Row 1	1,0	1,1	1,2	1,3
Row 2	2,0	2,1	2,2	2,3

Once you define the matrix, use the variables for these memory locations just like any other variable. If these cells represent safe deposit boxes, Illustration 6.6 reports on the value of the jewels locked in any one:

ILLUSTRATION 6.6

Double subscripts denote the row and column of a matrix item.

```
10 DIM A(2,3)
20 READ A(1,1), A(1,2), A(1,3)
30 READ A(2,1), A(2,2), A(2,3)
40 PRINT "ENTER THE ADDRESS OF YOUR SAFE DEPOSIT BOX"
50 INPUT "ROW"; R
60 INPUT "COLUMN"; C
70 PRINT "THE CONTENTS OF THE BOX IN ROW";R;"AND COLUMN" ;C;"ARE WORTH"
75 PRINT A(R,C);"DOLLARS"
80 DATA 200, 500000, 0,
90 DATA 999.99, 1000000, 45
100 END


RUN


ENTER THE ADDRESS OF YOUR SAFE DEPOSIT BOX
ROW? 2
COLUMN? 1
THE CONTENTS OF THE BOX IN ROW 2 COLUMN 1 ARE WORTH
999.99 DOLLARS
```

Lines 20 and 30 assign the numeric amounts in DATA to the variables in the matrix. The dollars in DATA and the variables in the READ are all carefully arranged to correspond with the value of the jewels in the actual arrangement of safe deposit boxes at the bank. Matrix A matches the vault shown in Illustration 6.7.

ILLUSTRATION 6.7

Central Bank vault

	Column 1	Column 2	Column 3
Row 1	$200	$500,000	0
Row 2	$999.99	$1,000,000	$45

When you enter row R and column C, for line 70, these variables become subscripts which PRINT uses to locate and retrieve the amounts stored in the double-subscript variable that represents cell R, C of the matrix.

Effective Use of Double Subscripts

Thus, just as with single subscripts, double subscripts can be variables or expressions. Once again, this makes it practical to store and search through large amounts of data because you can use the counting variable of a FOR . . . NEXT loop as a subscript. Use two loops because there are two subscripts.

Illustration 6.8 makes room reservations at a large resort hotel with 10 floors, each of which has 15 rooms. The illustration has three important sections: initialization, reservations, and output.

ILLUSTRATION 6.8

Double subscripts represent the floors and rooms of a hotel.

Initialization
```
10 DIM H$(10,15)
20 C = 0
30 FOR I = 1 TO 10
40     FOR J = 1 TO 15
50          H$(I,J) = "XXX"
60     NEXT J
70 NEXT I
```

Reservations
```
80 PRINT "WELCOME TO THE TROUTBROOKE HOTEL"
90 PRINT "WHICH ROOM DO YOU WANT?"
100 INPUT "FLOOR"; F
110 INPUT "ROOM"; R
120 IF H$(F,$) < > "XXX" THEN 180
130 PRINT "YOU MAY HAVE THAT ROOM"
140 INPUT "ENTER YOUR INITIALS"; H$(F,R)
150 C = C+1
160 IF C = 150 THEN 200
170 GO TO 80
180 PRINT "THAT ROOM IS RESERVED, TRY AGAIN"
190 GO TO 100
```

Output
```
200 PRINT "THE HOTEL IS FULL"
210 PRINT "HERE IS THE RESERVATION LIST"
215 PRINT
220 FOR I = 1 TO 10
230     FOR J = 1 TO 15
240          PRINT H$(I,J);"    ";
250     NEXT J
255 PRINT
260 NEXT I
270 END
```

Section 1 assigns XXX to every element of the H$(,) matrix that represents the hotel in the computer's memory. As reservations are made, this will be replaced by the initials of the hotel guest. Nested FOR . . . NEXT loops make it easy to manipulate the entire matrix. They are set up so that the inner loop, the J loop, represents the rooms on each floor. This loop runs completely for each of the 10 floors. The outer loop, the I loop, represents the 10 floors and RUNs to completion just once.

Section 2, lines 80 through 190, accepts reservations and uses the INPUT variables as subscripts for the H$(,) matrix variables to discover if the room is occupied. The IF . . . THEN check in line 120 determines whether the matrix variable still stores XXX. If so, the room is available. It is reserved when a guest's initials are entered in line 140.

The IF . . . THEN check in line 160 sets the final section in motion. When C (the counter that goes up by 1 each time a reservation is made) reaches 150, all of the rooms are occupied. Control goes ahead to line 200 and then to the nested FOR . . . NEXT loops that begin in line 220. They print the matrix as 10 rows each with 15 sets of initials.

Taking some time to enter Illustration 6.8 into the computer will clarify the use of double-subscripted variables. Use dummy names and watch it run. You should see something like Illustration 6.9 on your screen:

ILLUSTRATION 6.9

Running the program in Illustration 6.8 to reserve hotel rooms

```
RUN

WELCOME TO THE TROUTBROOKE HOTEL
WHICH ROOM DO YOU WANT?
FLOOR? 10
ROOM? 3
YOU MAY HAVE THAT ROOM
ENTER YOUR INITIALS? HMH
WELCOME TO THE TROUTBROOKE HOTEL
WHICH ROOM DO YOU WANT?
FLOOR 10
ROOM? 3
THAT ROOM IS RESERVED, TRY AGAIN
FLOOR? 5
ROOM? 5
```

```
YOU MAY HAVE THAT ROOM
                       .

                       .

      (eventually)
THE HOTEL IS FULL
HERE IS THE RESERVATION LIST

FDR JFK RFR LBJ GWK AWO ASW JMM HHM HBH KBH PLK SOC PDP TRS

IGR LPA TTY MFR HPL APL MSW BFG KNN NBM TGW ORD CCR MXM APP
                       .

                       .
```

      (and so on, with initials for 10 floors)
```
                       .

                       .
```

   By convention, I and J are used for subscripts in double-scripted matrices. In BASIC it is important to nest the loops so that the computer accesses the data across one row and then works on the next row. If it is forced to work down the columns, the computer takes much longer to access the entire matrix.

Problems

Corrections

1. In the spaces on the right, write "Correct" if the following BASIC statements are correct. If not, rewrite them correctly. Consider each statement separately. They are not part of the same program.

   a. `11 DIM A(40,10), B$(50)` _____

   b. `45 PRINT W(1,Y)` _____

   c. `35 DIM X(20,5)` _____

   d. `10 INPUT A$(X)` _____

   e. `60 DIM A$(60,80)` _____

f.   34 LET A(Y$) = INT(10*R+1) _____

g.   40 PRINT A(R(X)) _____

h.   35 A$(X) = T$ _____

i.   40 IF A$(Y) > A$(Y+1) THEN 100 _____

j.   50 PRINT X$(X+Z) _____

k.   20 A(3,4) = 50 _____

l.   35 DIM S(N) _____

m. 55 DIM F$(8*B) _____

n.   65 READ (5),(7),(9) _____

o.   34 DIM A(20,45), A$(12) = 85 _____

Program to read

2. If the digits 1 through 9 were input in ascending order to the program below, what would be the output?

```
10 LET T = 0
20 FOR A = 1 TO 3
30      FOR S = 1 TO 3
40            INPUT N(A,S)
50            T = T+N(A,S)
60      NEXT S
70 NEXT A
80 PRINT T, N(2,3)
90 END
```

Programs to write

3. A name and integer score is typed in at the terminal for each of the 50 golfers in the tournament. Make the computer print out a table showing each golfer's name, score, and how many scored higher.

4. A one-dimensional array named B contains 10 elements. Place the largest of these in G and the element number of G in E. Print out which element was the largest and exactly how large it was.

5. Use the computer to keep track of the use of computer facilities at the office computer center. There are 24 terminals available for staff

members. Keep a program running during one day that allows you to enter the number of users at each hour from 8:00 A.M. to 5:00 P.M. At the end of the day, have the computer print out a report giving the time (such as 8 A.M., 12 noon, and 3 P.M.) and the number of terminals in use at that hour.

6. The Best Bakery is so busy that each day it must receive deliveries of its 10 most needed ingredients: sugar, salt, yeast, butter, chocolate, flour, milk, vanilla, baking powder, and baking soda. Write the program that runs all day and accepts the inventory number of the items that are delivered. At the end of the deliveries have the computer print out the list of goods not delivered so that the errand boy can do some emergency shopping.

7. The fourth-graders are reluctant to dress differently from their classmates. Use the computer to help pick out three colors that all will wear today. Select them at random from a list of 10 possible colors.

8. The Flower Farm wants to spur its five packing employees to greater productivity. At the end of the week the number of boxes packed by each person on each day will be entered into the computer. The computer will then calculate and print:
   a. The average of boxes packed in one day
   b. The highest number packed by one person
   c. The employee number and the day that the top packer achieved such success

9. The Wrestling League gives awards to individual wrestlers as well as to the championship team. Write the program that the league chairman can use to enter the season's points for each wrestler in the league (each team has five wrestlers). Have it print out the top five wrestlers and their team name. Assume that this league has only two teams: North High and South High.

10. Write the program that keeps track of reservations on the Speedy Piper Cub Airways' only plane. It has four rows of three seats each. Whenever a seat is reserved, store the initials of the passenger for that seat. When the plane is full, print out the seating chart:

```
BJK HHM JMM
TTY KBL JAM
MMM VAA ACM
RAM ROM IBM
```

Chapter 7

Subroutines and Functions

Perhaps you can imagine that writing a computer program to solve truly complex problems is quite time-consuming. Yet fancy programs that allow computer novices to store and analyze large amounts of diverse data are commonplace. Their use is routine, particularly in the business world.

Professional programmers, however, are constantly facing deadlines. Rarely is one granted the freedom from time constraints often enjoyed by the creative artist; a programmer's life is more akin to that of an emergency medical technician. Some programmers traverse their territory in radio-equipped vehicles, diagnosing and correcting problems and continually modifying their programs for new users. To do the job well, one must be quick as well as competent.

The key to professional success is to develop a "bag of tricks" that can be called upon as situations arise. Routines that search through double-subscripted matrices or format reports, for example, are always handy. For every new problem, wise programmers develop general solutions that can be transplanted rather than create ingenious but unique solutions.

Even if you'll never duplicate your program, you should work with distinct program segments. Like building with blocks, each one can be tested and made secure before the next one is added. Then, even if your final product is enormous, you know it works because its components are sound.

Program modules save time and space when you want to use one routine several times in the same program. Rather than duplicating it, write a single program segment that you reference over and over again.

BASIC makes it easy to build such program modules. This chapter presents three useful techniques for doing so: subroutines, programmer-defined functions, and error traps. It also discusses the ON . . . GO SUB and the ON . . . GO TO statements that help implement these techniques.

Subroutines: The GO SUB and the RETURN Statements

GO SUB is a fancy GO TO statement that not only sends control to the specified subroutine line, but also remembers which GO SUB statement caused this branching. When the subroutine is completed, control is sent back to the line following the most recently executed GO SUB statement, and processing continues in the usual sequential manner. The RETURN statement makes this return trip happen.

Illustration 7.1 uses a subroutine to help print college course announcements.

ILLUSTRATION 7.1

Using GO SUB and RETURN for repeated use of a program segment

```
10 PRINT "BASIC WOODWORKING"
20 PRINT "M W F 3-6 PM"
30 PRINT "PROFESSOR KNIFE"
40 GO SUB 1000
50 PRINT "INTERMEDIATE WOODWORKING"
60 PRINT "TU TH SAT 9-11 AM"
70 PRINT "PROFESSOR SAW"
80 GO SUB 1000
90 PRINT "ADVANCED WOODWORKING"
100 PRINT "SUNDAY ONLY 9-5"
110 PRINT "PROFESSOR POWER"
120 GO TO 1100
1000 PRINT "COLLEGE OF USEFUL SKILLS"
1010 PRINT "TREEMONT STREET"
```

```
1020 PRINT "WOODSTOCK, TX"
1030 PRINT
1040 PRINT
1050 RETURN
1100 END

RUN

BASIC WOODWORKING
M W F 3-6 PM
PROFESSOR KNIFE
COLLEGE OF USEFUL SKILLS
TREEMONT STREET
WOODSTOCK, TX

INTERMEDIATE WOODWORKING
TU TH SAT 9-11 AM
PROFESSOR SAW
COLLEGE OF USEFUL SKILLS
TREEMONT STREET
WOODSTOCK, TX

ADVANCED WOODWORKING
SUNDAY ONLY 9-5
PROFESSOR POWER
COLLEGE OF USEFUL SKILLS
TREEMONT STREET
WOODSTOCK, TX
```

Lines 1000 through 1050 are the subroutine. Lines 10 through 110 are the main routine, and line 120 separates the two. The subroutine facility has greatly improved the programmer's efficiency. Unique details are coded in the main routine. Those which may be repeated for each course are coded only once in the subroutine and used as often as necessary.

The separation created by line 120 ensures that the subroutine is activated only at the appropriate times by the GO SUB statements carefully placed in the main routine. The computer gives an error message if it encounters a RETURN without first executing a corresponding GO SUB statement.

Illustration 7.2 uses a subroutine to search through a list of foods and retrieve their caloric value. It illustrates, in a simple way, the use of a subroutine to transplant a prewritten routine in modular form. This programmer chooses to reserve lines 500 through 530 for a search routine (developed over years of experience!). If it is needed, as in this illustration, the main routine and the DATA which establish details particular to this project are coded in other line numbers. The search routine is "plugged in" when lines 500 through 530 are copied from the programmer's library of useful techniques.

ILLUSTRATION 7.2

Plugging a prewritten subroutine into reserved program lines

```
10 INPUT "WHAT FRUIT DO YOU LIKE"; F$
20 GO SUB 500
30 PRINT "EACH ";F$; " HAS"; X; " CALORIES"
40 GO TO 550
500 READ X$, X
510 IF X$ = F$ THEN 530
520 GO TO 500
530 RETURN
535 DATA APRICOT, 18, CANTALOUPE, 120, FIG, 60
540 DATA PEACH, 35, PLUM, 25, WATERMELON, 1840
550 END

RUN

WHAT FRUIT DO YOU LIKE? PLUM
EACH PLUM HAS 25 CALORIES

WHAT FRUIT DO YOU LIKE? WATERMELON
EACH WATERMELON HAS 1840 CALORIES
```

Notice that the subroutine uses the data in DATA statements outside the routine itself. It also uses and understands the variable F$ which was defined by the INPUT statement in line 10. Even though they are distinct segments, subroutines are integral parts of a program.

Subroutines can call other subroutines and thus be nested as many times as the memory capacity of your computer allows. The real limitation in such a scheme is the clarity of your logic. Keep the relationship among your subroutines and between them and the main routine as clear as possible.

On the IBM personal computer, the RETURN statement may include a line number to designate where to pass control when subroutine processing completes. Use this facility only for special "event trapping" routines and not for usual subroutines. RETURN (line) allows subroutines to handle responses to an event such as the touch of a light pen or the trigger of a joystick by returning control to the input routine to wait for another event. Such subroutines actually reverse the normal use of a subroutine where the destination after each pass through the routine differs. In normal subroutines you do not want RETURN to have a line number; you want to take advantage of its ability to follow the flow of program execution.

The ON . . . GO TO and the ON . . . GO SUB Statements

Both of these statements enable branching to one of several possible lines in a program and are very useful in controlling the flow of programs developed in the modular style. Consider, for example, a program that has three separate modules which execute depending on whether the user placed first, second, or third, in the City Marathon. ON . . . GO TO helps in this simplified version of the project (Illustration 7.3).

ILLUSTRATION 7.3

ON . . . GO TO sets the direction of program control.

```
10 INPUT "ENTER YOUR FINISHING PLACE"; X
20 ON X GO TO 60, 70, 80
30 PRINT "ONLY THE TOP THREE RUNNERS, PLEASE"
40 GO TO 10
60 PRINT "CONGRATULATIONS! YOU GET THE GOLD MEDAL!"
65 GO TO 99
70 PRINT "TAKE THE SILVER MEDAL"
75 GO TO 99
80 PRINT "TAKE THE BRONZE MEDAL!"
99 END

RUN

ENTER YOUR FINISHING PLACE? 3
TAKE THE BRONZE MEDAL!

RUN
```

ENTER YOUR FINISHING PLACE? 10
ONLY THE TOP THREE RUNNERS, PLEASE

The program expects X to be either 1, 2, or 3, a value that corresponds to a position in the list of line numbers in line 20. The computer will branch to the Xth line number in the list. When the user entered 3, control jumped to the bronze medal "module" in line 80. If X is zero or higher than the number of line numbers, control defaults to line 40, the next line.

Any arithmetic expression may be used in place of X. The computer will round the final value of the expression to the nearest integer and then decide where to send control. ON . . . GO SUB works exactly the same as ON . . . GO TO, except that a subroutine is the destination of the branch. When a RETURN statement executes in the subroutine, the computer branches back to the line following the ON . . . GO SUB statement.

FNA( ) is a function like SQR( ) and INT( ) that the programmer of Illustration 7.4 has written. The DEF FN statement

The DEF FN Statement

ILLUSTRATION 7.4

A user-defined function

```
10 DEF FNA(X) = X*7
20 PRINT "ENTER THE AGE OF YOUR PET DOG"
30 INPUT D
40 PRINT "IF YOUR DOG WERE HUMAN"
50 PRINT "IT WOULD BE"
60 PRINT FNA(D)
70 PRINT "YEARS OLD"
80 END

RUN

ENTER THE AGE OF YOUR PET DOG
? 4
IF YOUR DOG WERE HUMAN
IT WOULD BE
28
YEARS OLD
```

in line 10 DEFines it for the program. This is the prototype the computer uses when it encounters FNA( ) elsewhere in the program. Then the computer applies the same actions to the real argument as the DEF FN statement applies to its dummy argument. In the illustration, X, the dummy argument, is multiplied by 7. Thus, when FNA( ) uses a real argument, D, in line 60, the value of D is also multiplied by 7.

Of course, DEF statements are normally used to define much more complicated relationships. An exteme example of this is the DEF statement below. It is taken from a program that analyzes survey results:

```
10 DEF FNE(Y) = INT(ABS(9-Y) + SQR(Y-W) - INT(ABS(Y-INT(X))))
```

Programmer-defined function names like FNA in Illustration 7.4 must be made of FN and any legal variable. The function definition can be located anywhere in a program, but must occur before the

function name is used to call the function. Usually a separate section of line numbers at the beginning is reserved for function definitions. If they exist in a program, these functions can be called in the same situations as the usual computer supplied functions: in PRINT statements or LET statements or wherever arithmetic operations are allowed.

Programmer-defined functions may also be string functions, as shown in Illustration 7.5.

ILLUSTRATION 7.5

A programmer-defined string function

```
10 DEF FNC$(N$) = N$ + "LY"
20 INPUT "GIVE ME AN ADJECTIVE"; V$
30 PRINT "HERE IS THE ADVERB"
40 PRINT FNC$(V$)
50 END

RUN


GIVE ME AN ADJECTIVE? QUICK
HERE IS THE ADVERB
QUICKLY
```

Line 10 tells the computer to add LY to any string given as the argument of the function FNC$. This occurs in line 40. String functions have string variables appended to their name; the arguments are strings, and the result is, not surprisingly, a character string.

There may be several arguments specified in the DEF statement. The function in Illustration 7.6 calculates volumes and requires three numeric arguments.

ILLUSTRATION 7.6

DEF may have several dummy arguments.

```
10 DEF FNV(X,Y,Z) = X*Y*Z
20 INPUT "ENTER THE HEIGHT, WIDTH, LENGTH"; H,W,L
30 S = FNV(H,W,L)
40 PRINT "THE VOLUME OF THE BOX IS:"; S
50 END

RUN
```

```
ENTER THE HEIGHT, WIDTH, LENGTH? 3,4,5
THE VOLUME OF THE BOX IS: 60
```

Be sure that the real arguments used when the function is called agree in number and data type (strings or numbers) with the dummy arguments in the DEF FN statement.

The ON ERROR GO TO Statement

Error traps are special subroutines that prevent the automatic stopping of a program each time an error occurs. They determine if an error is one of a few that concern you. If so, the error-handling subroutine takes the corrective measures you specify and returns control to the main routine. If the error is not one of particular interest, control returns to the computer which handles the error in the usual way.

Illustration 7.7 catches the subscript out-of-range error and prints a scolding message. Other errors are handled in the normal manner.

Line 10 ensures that whenever an error occurs, control will jump to the first line of the error-handling routine. This line, line 80, checks the ERR variable that contains the code number of the error. If it is not for the error that interests you, the ON ERROR GO TO 0 statement tells the computer to handle the error in the usual fashion. If it is, control falls into the routine where the user is scolded and asked to try again. Resume 30 in line 110 at the end of the error trap sends control back to the INPUT statement.

ILLUSTRATION 7.7

Trapping for subscript-out-of-range

```
10 ON ERROR GO TO 80
20 DIM A(3)
25 READ A(1), A(2), A(3)
30 INPUT "WHICH SCORE DO YOU WANT"; N
40 PRINT A(N); "IS THE SCORE FOR #"; N
45 DATA 34,56,69
50 GO TO 999
80 IF ERR <> 9 THEN ON ERROR GO TO 0
90 PRINT
100 PRINT "ONLY 3 CHOICES, TRY AGAIN"
110 RESUME 30
999 END
```

```
RUN

WHICH SCORE DO YOU WANT? 3
 69 IS THE SCORE FOR # 3
OK


RUN

WHICH SCORE DO YOU WANT? 8

ONLY 3 CHOICES, TRY AGAIN
WHICH SCORE DO YOU WANT? 1
 34 IS THE SCORE FOR # 1
OK
```

The RESUME Statement

All error traps should execute a RESUME statement. This tells the computer that the most recent error has been handled, that the error condition flag should be turned off, and that processing should proceed. RESUME 0 or RESUME, alone, sends control back to the line where the error occurred. This is appropriate if your error-handling routine does something to correct the problem. RESUME NEXT sends control back to the line following the one where the error occurred. And, as Illustration 7.7 shows, RESUME with a line number sends control to the line you specify. RESUME NEXT and RESUME (line) allow your program to continue regardless of whether you correct the error.

Not all computer errors can be trapped and handled by a computer program. Trappable errors are related to common programmer and user mistakes such as arithmetic miscalculations (Overflow), incorrect programming (FOR without NEXT), and input/output errors (Out of paper). Illustration 7.8 is a complete list of the error codes and their messages.

The ERROR Statement

You can set up your own error code number, between 0 and 255, and test for these values in your error-handling routine as well as for the system error codes. The ERROR statement makes this possible.

When an ERROR statement executes, the computer functions as though a real error has occurred. If your program has one, control passes to an error-handling routine; otherwise, the computer

ILLUSTRATION 7.8

Error codes

ERR number	Message	ERR number	Message
1	NEXT without FOR	26	FOR without NEXT
2	Syntax error	27	Out of paper
3	RETURN without GOSUB	29	WHILE without WEND
4	Out of data	30	WEND without WHILE
5	Illegal function call	50	FIELD overflow
6	Overflow	51	Internal error
7	Out of memory	52	Bad file number
8	Undefined line number	53	File not found
9	Subscript out of range	54	Bad file mode
10	Duplicate definition	55	File already open
11	Division by zero	57	Device I/O error
12	Illegal direct	58	File already exists
13	Type mismatch	61	Disk full
14	Out of string space	62	Input past end
15	String too long	63	Bad record number
16	String formula too complex	64	Bad file name
17	Can't continue	66	Direct statement in file
18	Undefined user function	67	Too many files
19	No RESUME	68	Device unavailable
20	RESUME without error	69	Communication buffer overflow
21	Unprintable error	70	Disk write protect
22	Missing operand	71	Disk not ready
23	Line buffer overflow	72	Disk media error
24	Device timeout	73	Advanced feature
25	Device fault		

prints the error message associated with the error code given in the ERROR statement.

```
50 ERROR 2
```

assigns error code number 2 to the ERR variable and makes the computer respond as though a syntax error had occurred.

The great value of the ERROR statement is that you can give any code number in the range of 0 to 255. That means you can make up your own error codes. When control reaches the error-handling routine, your code will have been assigned to ERR and can be recognized by the routine just as the regular BASIC error codes are recognized. Illustration 7.9 uses error code 200 to send control to an error-handling routine. When the ERROR statement appended to IF . . . THEN in line 55 executes, control passes to the error-handling routine that begins in line 100. The computer uses the PRINT statement in line 110 as the error message to inform the user that he has lost his turn at bat.

If an ERROR statement executes in a program that has no error-handling routine, the computer tries to print a message associated with the error code. When there is none, the computer complains with the message: Unprintable error.

ILLUSTRATION 7.9

Programmer-defined ERR codes

```
10 ON ERROR GO TO 100
20 X = 0
30 INPUT "HOW FAR IS THE MOON"; FAR
40 IF FAR <> 238857.0! THEN 50
45 PRINT "GOOD FOR YOU"
48 GO TO 130
50 X = X+1
55 IF X > 2 THEN ERROR 200
60 GO TO 30
100 IF ERR <> 200 THEN ON ERROR GO TO 0
110 PRINT "THREE STRIKES AND YOU'RE OUT!"
120 RESUME 130
130 END

RUN

HOW FAR IS THE MOON? 500000
HOW FAR IS THE MOON? 10000
HOW FAR IS THE MOON? 689999
THREE STRIKES AND YOU'RE OUT!
OK
```

Problems

Corrections

1. In the spaces on the right, write "Correct" if the following BASIC statements are correct. If not, rewrite them correctly. Consider each statement separately. These statements are not part of the same program.

    a. 35 RETURN 100 _____

    b. 100 DEF FNP(M) _____

    c. 84 ON S GO SUB 100,100,500,800 _____

    d. 22 FNA _____

    e. 98 GO SUB _____

    f. 66 FNA = 9 _____

    g. 56 RETURN _____

    h. 71 DEF FNB(A,B,C) _____

    i. 6675 DEF FNP = X^2 − 2*X+1 _____

    j. 15 FNS = Y _____

2. In the spaces on the right, write ''Correct'' if the following BASIC statements are correct. If not, rewrite them correctly. Consider each statement separately. These statements are not part of the same program.

    a. 12 DEF FNP(X) = X*4 _____

    b. 11 ON X$ GO TO 100,200,300 _____

    c. 35 FNS _____

    d. 54 ON X GO TO 80, 90, 100 _____

    e. 88 GO SUB 123 _____

    f. 10 ON ERROR RESUME _____

    g. 45 RESUME _____

    h. 56 ON ERROR GO TO 0 _____

    i. 67 ON ERR GO TO 100 _____

    j. ON S GO SUB _____

Programs to read

3.
```
120 FOR I = 1 TO 3
130     FOR J = 1 TO 4
140         PRINT "GL";
150         ON I GO TO 160,180,200
160         PRINT "A";
170         GO TO 210
180         PRINT "E";
190         GO TO 210
200         PRINT "I";
210         ON J GO TO 220,240,250,270
220         PRINT "S",
230         GO TO 2600
240         PRINT "P",
245         GO TO 2600
250         PRINT "T",
260         GO TO 2600
270         PRINT "R"
2600    NEXT J
2610    PRINT
2620 NEXT I
2630 END
```

4.
```
10 DEF FNP(A) = A^2-2*A-1
20 PRINT "X", "FNP(X)"
30 FOR X = 1 TO 5
40     PRINT X, FNP(X)
50 NEXT X
60 END
```

Programs to write

5. Write a computer program that gives a quiz on all of the multiplication tables from 1 to 12. Use a subroutine to print out responses to each user's answer. If the answer is correct, give a cheery response. If the answer is wrong, be negative. In order to make the quiz more interesting, store several cheery answers and several negative ones and randomly pick which one will be used. Keep a count of the number of correct answers and report the final score.

6. Write a computer quiz with 10 questions on any topic you choose. Make the computer seem more "human" by varying its response to the user's answers. Each time an answer is correct, have the computer pick a cheery reply from several choices in a DATA statement. Each

time an answer is incorrect, randomly pick a negative response from DATA.

7. Use the computer to give advice to tennis players. Ask 10 questions that will show their knowledge of the game. If they answer zero questions correctly, have the computer question their ability to read; if they get fewer than 3 correct, print out TRY ANOTHER SPORT; if they get 4–6 correct, print out the basic rules of the game; if they get 7–9 correct, print out tips to improve their game; and if they get all 10 correct, give them a list of important tennis tournaments to play in.

8. Once a person knows how to operate a particular program, it is boring to see the instructions each time it runs. Write a routine that may be included in other programs, which asks if the user wishes to see instructions. If so, send control to a subroutine that prints them out.

9. Assume that the following statements were executed in a BASIC program:

```
100 ON ERROR GO TO 1000
110 INPUT A%
```

The user types in 75000. Write an IF statement at the appropriate line number to trap this error (overflow), print a message that informs the user that the number is too large, and re-execute the INPUT statement.

10. Write an error-trapping routine that recognizes an Out of Data error, takes whatever action you feel is appropriate, and ends the program. Test your error trap in a sample program.

Chapter 8

String Functions and Print Formats

Computer recording of checking account transactions has done a great deal to speed up bank procedures, reduce errors, and save money. Nevertheless, checking account patrons at one bank were not pleased when the transition to computer accounting occurred. Rather than getting a handwritten receipt for their deposits stating the date, the account number, and the amount, they received a computer-printed receipt like the one in Illustration 8.1.

This receipt is very hard to read. If you study it carefully, you may figure out that a deposit of $300.00 was made to account 410667. But you will probably have to ask someone at the bank to help you find the date. It is among the rightmost characters

ILLUSTRATION 8.1

Computer-printed bank deposit receipt

DEPOSITS ARE ACCEPTED SUBJECT TO VERIFICATION FOR ACCURACY.

This bank symbol, transaction number, date and amount of your deposit are shown below

410667≠aS   ₂₆S₆T₈ 883   30000=aS527₈₈

THANK YOU FOR THIS DEPOSIT
ALWAYS OBTAIN THIS OFFICIAL RECEIPT WHEN MAKING A DEPOSIT

and is composed of digits written both sideways and normally: 01-27-83 for January 27, 1983.

Illustration 8.1 shows how frustrating a poorly designed computer printout can be and underscores the fact that the print and screen designs which program users face are ambassadors for the genius and usefulness of the programmer's work. Frequently they determine how often a program will be used, or if, in fact, it will be used at all. Where they have a choice, users will certainly select a program that does less but is clear before one that is more powerful but cryptic.

One of the great strengths of BASIC is that it makes it easy to create clear, "user-oriented" input and output routines. This chapter presents the string functions and the PRINT TAB( ), PRINT US-ING, and LPRINT USING statements that make such friendly and effective programs possible.

String Functions

String-handling functions are among the most powerful BASIC formatting tools. They add flexibility and effectiveness to both input and output by bridging the gap between the variety of human responses and the rigid numerical codes of the computer.

Illustration 8.2 shows how string functions make life a great deal easier for the wrestling coach who must enter match results for all of the wrestlers in all of the weight classes for every team in the league. Because the string handlers in lines 20 through 60 interpret his entries, all he needs to do is to enter an unbroken preplanned string to describe each wrestler. For example, JONES110P4.5 means that Jones in the 110-weight class pinned his opponent in four-and-a-half minutes.

ILLUSTRATION 8.2

Using string functions to retrieve key portions of a lengthy string

```
10  INPUT "ENTER RESULTS FOR ONE MAN";R$
20  N$ = LEFT$(R$,5)
30  W$ = MID$(R$,6,3)
40  D$ = MID$(R$,9,1)
50  T$ = RIGHT$(R$,3)
60  T = VAL(T$)
70  PRINT "NAME"; N$
```

```
80 PRINT "WEIGHT CLASS"; W$
90 PRINT "DECISION"; D$
100 PRINT "TIME"; T
110 END

RUN

ENTER RESULTS FOR ONE MAN? JONES110P4.5
NAME JONES
WEIGHT CLASS 110
DECISION P
TIME 4.5
```

R$ becomes JONES110P4.5
N$ becomes 5 lefthand characters R$
W$ becomes 3 middle characters of R$ starting at character 6
D$ becomes 1 middle character of R$ starting at character 9
T$ becomes the 3 rightmost characters of R$
T   becomes the string digits of T$ converted to numeric digits

 LEFT$, MID$, RIGHT$, VAL are examples of string function names. The arguments in this illustration are constants or variables, but they may also be expressions. String function results (JONES, 110, P, and 4.5) may be character strings or numbers. String functions appear in the same context as arithmetic ones: in LET, PRINT, and other statements where arithmetic expressions occur. The string handlers that are available differ among computers. Illustration 8.3 shows how the most commonly used functions are written on the IBM personal computer.

Formatting Output

You have probably already discovered the limitations of the PRINT statement. One problem is that using a comma gives you only a few horizontal tab positions: five in text or high-resolution, two in medium-resolution. Another problem is that it prints numbers with as much precision as possible and left-justifies them in the print field. Using PRINT to create a report of utility costs produces something like Illustration 8.4.

 These numbers are really not suitable for dollar amounts and are very hard to read if you wish to compare categories. You need to line up the decimal points, round off the decimal positions, append zeros on the right and, possibly, include dollar signs.

ILLUSTRATION 8.3

String functions (X$ = "VALENTINE")

Command	Result
LEFT$(X$,4)	"VALE"
MID$(X$,6,3)	"TIN"
RIGHT$(X$,6)	"ENTINE"
LEN(X$)	9
ASC(X$)	86
CHR$(86)	"V"
STR$(86)	"86"
VAL("86")	86

LEFT$(X$,X)	Extracts the first X characters from the string X$.
MID$(X$,X,Y)	Extracts a substring Y characters long beginning at the Xth character in X$.
RIGHT$(X$,X)	Extracts the X rightmost characters of X$.
LEN(X$)	Produces a number that is the count of the number of characters in X$.
ASC(X$)	Produces a number that is the ASCII code equivalent of the first character in X$.
CHR$(X)	Produces a character that has the ASCII code X.
SPACE$(X)	Produces a string of X blank spaces.
STR$(X)	Produces a string of digits that are the digits in the number X.
VAL(X$)	The opposite of STR$. Produces a number made up of the digits in X$ unless the digits are preceded by nonnumeric characters, in which case zero is returned.

ILLUSTRATION 8.4

Utility costs

Water	45.176
Electricity	125
Telephone	9.56
Heat	.81

The computer has several facilities for doing these things; some are more powerful than others. PRINT TAB( ) allows you to control horizontal spacing. PRINT USING reformats numbers and character strings.

The PRINT TAB( ) Statement

The argument in parentheses determines the position on the print line where printing begins. The statement:

```
10 PRINT TAB(20); "MARATHON"
```

prints MARATHON beginning in position 20 of the print line. You can specify as many tab positions as you find useful in one PRINT TAB( ) statement. The only rule is that you cannot ask the computer to reverse direction and print to the left of a position already printed. Thus,

```
10 PRINT TAB(12); "FIRST"; TAB(22); 7.65
```

places FIRST beginning in position 12 and 7.65 beginning in position 23. (The computer always prints numbers with a leading space for a minus sign.)

You may specify up to PRINT TAB(255) even though one print line has no more than 80 print positions. The computer will count beyond the end of one line onto the next if it needs to. If you specify a position to the left of the current cursor, the computer will skip to that position on the next line.

Using variables and arithmetic expressions as the argument in PRINT TAB( ) allows you to use this statement to make graphs. Illustration 8.5 prints the graph of Y = X as X goes from 1 to 5. Since printing scrolls up the screen, the top of the graph must be printed first. Thus, the FOR . . . NEXT loop in lines 10 through 60 generates the X values in descending order.

ILLUSTRATION 8.5

Using PRINT TAB( ) for graphing

```
10 FOR X = 5 TO 1 STEP −1
20    PRINT TAB(6+(3*X)); "*"
30    FOR Y = 1 TO (2*X) − (2*(X−1)−1)
40        PRINT
50    NEXT Y
```

```
60 NEXT X
70 PRINT "X VALUES:";
80 FOR X = 1 TO 5
90    PRINT X;
100 NEXT X
110 END

RUN


                   *
                 *
               *
             *
           *
X VALUES: 1 2 3 4 5
```

PRINT TAB( ) in line 20 calculates the horizontal position of the asterisk that denotes the function value. It allows for a six-character offset at the left margin and three print positions for each mark (space, asterisk, space).

The nested FOR . . . NEXT loop in lines 30 through 50 determines the slope of the graph. It calculates the number of print lines between the asterisk just printed and the next. To do this, it finds the current function value $(2*X)$ and subtracts the next value $(2*(X-1))$. Finally, it reduces the result by 1 to take into account the print line of the asterisk itself.

Lines 70 through 100 print the bottom line of the graph. These PRINT statements end with a semicolon to keep their output all on one line.

TAB( ) is actually a function on the IBM personal computer. It can also be used with the LPRINT and PRINT# (explained in Chapter 13) statements.

The PRINT USING Statement

PRINT USING requires two pieces of information: which print format to use and which information to display using the format. The format and the data are separated by a semicolon. Either field, the format specification or the data, can contain constants or be represented by variables. Illustration 8.6 uses both alternatives to demonstrate PRINT USING.

ILLUSTRATION 8.6

PRINT USING

With constants	With variables
| ```
10 PRINT USING "####,.#";4532.67
20 END
``` | ```
10 F$ = "####,.#"
20 F = 4532.67
30 PRINT USING F$;F
40 END
``` |
| RUN | RUN |
| 4,532.7 | 4,532.7 |

The format specification is a string in which some characters have special meaning. In Illustration 8.6 each number sign (#) represents a place for one digit. The comma to the left of the decimal point in the format specification tells the computer to insert a comma in the output before every three digits left of the decimal point. The decimal point in the format specification shows the placement of the decimal for the output. If, as in the illustration, the number to be printed has more decimal places than the specification, the number will be rounded to fit the specification. All of the format specifiers available to you are listed in Illustration 8.7.

ILLUSTRATION 8.7

PRINT USING format specifiers

Symbol	Functions	Examples	
# (number sign)	To indicate a numeric field. Each # represents space for one digit. If the number is short, it is preceded on the left by blanks. If the number has too many integer positions it is printed with a preceding %, denoting an error.	Constant: Format: Result:	546 "####" 546
. (dot)	To indicate the position of the decimal point in a numeric field. Numbers with more decimal digits than the format allows will be rounded. Right-hand zeros are appended to numbers with fewer decimal digits.	Constant: Format: Result:	345.6712 "###.##" 345.67

Symbol	Functions	Examples	
, . (comma/decimal)	To indicate that commas will be inserted in a numeric field every three digits to the left of the decimal point. A comma at the right of a format appears at the right of the output.	Constant: Format: Result:	934582 "###,.###" 934,582
$$ (dollar signs)	To indicate that a "$" will precede a numeric field. The $ will "float" to the character position preceding the number. The symbols account for two positions in the field: one for the $ and one for a digit. A single $ will not "float" but will appear as placed in the format.	Constant: Format: Result:	581.75 "$$##.##" $581.75
** (asterisks)	To indicate that unused left-hand positions in a numeric field will be filled with *. These count as two additional # positions in the field.	Constant: Format: Result:	7650.1 "**######.##" ****7650.10
^^^^ (carets)	To indicate that the number will be printed in the exponential format. The four characters allow for the E-xx positions that follow the significant digits.	Constant: Format: Result:	10000 ".#^^^^" .1E05
− (trailing minus)	To indicate that the minus sign will be printed to the right of a negative number.	Constant: Format: Result:	−56 "###−" 56−
+ (plus sign)	To indicate that the number will be signed. A plus or a minus will be printed when appropriate.	Constant: Format: Result:	−4 "+#" −4
\ \ (back-slashes)	To indicate a string field. Both the symbols and the spaces between them count as space for one character.	Constant: Format: Result:	SPARKLE "\ \" SPARKLE
& (ampersand)	To indicate a variable length string field. The data will be printed as it is.	Constant: Format: Result:	SPARKLE "&" SPARKLE
! (exclamation)	To indicate printing of the first character of a string.	Constant: Format: Result:	SAND "!" S
− (underscore)	To indicate that the next character should be printed as it literally is.	Constant: Format: Result:	4.5 "#.#_%" 4.5%
	Any other characters in the format descriptor are printed as literal character strings.	Constant: Format: Result:	4 "A = #" A = 4

Illustration 8.8 shows how PRINT USING provides the solution to the problem posed at the outset of this section on formatting: how to print a table of expenditures for certain utilities.

ILLUSTRATION 8.8

```
10 PRINT TAB(7); "UTILITY COSTS"
20 F$ = "\           \      $$,###,.##"
30 FOR X = 1 TO 4
40     READ A$, A
50     PRINT USING F$; A$; A
60 NEXT X
70 DATA WATER, 45.176
80 DATA ELECTRICITY, 125
90 DATA TELEPHONE, 9.56
100 DATA HEAT, .81
110 END


RUN

        UTILITY COSTS
WATER            $45.18
ELECTRICITY     $125.00
TELEPHONE         $9.56
HEAT              $0.81
```

Notice line 50. The format specifier F$ is followed by a list of items to be printed according to its design. The computer takes these items in sequence and fits them into the plan of the format specification. Notice that the data that the PRINT USING statement organizes matches the number and type of descriptive fields in the format specification: a character string followed by a number.

Illustration 8.8 produces a report with the decimal points lined up and the numerical amounts presented as dollars and cents. It is the kind of printout a computer user will find helpful.

The LPRINT USING Statement

This statement works exactly as the PRINT USING statement does except that the printing occurs on the printer. The print line should be set for 80 characters. Do this by entering:

```
WIDTH "LPT1:",80
```

Problems

Corrections

1. In the spaces on the right, write "Correct" if the following BASIC statements are correct. If not, rewrite them correctly. Consider each statement separately. These statements are not part of the same program.

   a. 80 PRINT TAB(X); X _____

   b. 77 PRINT TAB(24); "TITLE" _____

   c. 20 VAL(M$) = V$ _____

   d. 12 ON LEN(A$) GO TO 10,20,30 _____

   e. 31 ON VAL(X$) GO SUB 100,200,300 _____

   f. 48 IF LEN(A$,2) = 16 THEN 100 _____

   g. 23 T$ = LEFT(V$,3,4) _____

   h. 56 M$ = MID(F$) _____

   i. 23 IF MID(X$, 1, 2) = 495 THEN 56 _____

   j. 55 LEN D$ = 16 _____

Programs to read

In the space on the right, write what will be printed when the following programs are RUN. If input is required, give an example that would make sense to the program.

```
2. 10 A$ = "PALINDROME"
   20 PRINT LEFT$(A$,2)
   30 PRINT RIGHT$(A$,2)
   40 PRINT MID$(A$,7,4)
   50 PRINT LEN(A$)
   60 END

3. 10 A$ = "35 HORSES"
   20 X = VAL(LEFT$(A$,2))
   30 PRINT 2*X
   40 END
```

```
4. 10  V$ = "\        \        \        \"
   20  PRINT "REPORT ON WAGES"
   30  READ N$, W$
   40  PRINT USING V$;N$;W$
   50  GO TO 30
   60  DATA HERPIN, 4.25, BARTRAM, 4.75, DRISCOLL, 3.85
   70  END
```

Programs to write

5. Write the computer program that prints out the mailing labels for the Department Store catalog. Use the customers' name, street, city, and zip code stored in DATA statements.

6. A line of input is typed at the terminal. It begins at the left margin and ends before the right margin with a period and contains no other punctuation. It is, in fact, a one-line sentence. Make the computer print how many words are in the sentence.

7. A *palindrome* is a word or number which reads the same backward or forward. The word "Otto" is a palindrome. Program the computer to see if a line of input is a palindrome. Have it accept the input, test it, and then print out: THAT IS A PALINDROME or THAT IS NOT A PALINDROME.

8. Write a program that produces a table with the title:

   ```
   THE ASCII CODE FOR CAPITAL LETTERS
   ```

   Include in the table both the decimal ASCII value and the capital letters it represents.

9. Often a program gives a user a choice as to whether he or she wants the program to run again or stop. Write this routine, which might be added to any program. Give users the freedom to answer the query "Do you wish to play again?" with "Yes" or "Yeah" or "Yep" or any word beginning with *Y*. If they do, send control back to the beginning of the program. Otherwise, stop.

10. Computers are used to flash the special messages high above Times Square. Write the New Year's Eve program that counts down the last 60 seconds of the old year and then print out:

    ```
    HAPPY
     NEW
    YEAR
    ```

    Make each letter from several small ones, e.g., a large *H* from several normal sized *H*'s, a large *A* from several smaller *A*'s, and so forth.

11. Computers run the fancy scoreboards in many of the sports arenas around the country. Write the program for the Three Rivers Stadium in Pittsburgh that keeps track of the Steelers' football games. Have it accept information about the score for each team, the quarter being played, the down coming up, and the yards to go to make a first down. Then flash these statistics on the terminal "scoreboard." Remember, putting in the data should be quick and easy for the user:

    0741308

    to signify 07 points for the home team, 14 for the visitors, 1 for the first quarter, 3 for the down, and 8 yards to go. String functions can separate each element of the input for use by the program.

12. Nutritionists have discovered that kittens need 1½ ounces of Katty Food each day in order to grow at a healthy rate. Each ounce of this food contains the following amounts of essential nutrients: protein, 2 mg; vitamin A, 10 mg; vitamin C, 15 mg; and iron, 9 mg. Use PRINT USING to produce a report like the one below, which tells how much of each nutrient 1½ ounces of Katty Food provides.

    ```
    OUNCES REQUIRED TO GROW
    PROTEIN        3.0
    VIT. A        15.0
    VIT. C        22.5
    IRON          13.5
    ```

Part Four

Special Features

Chapter 9

Structured Programming: The Computer Dating Example

Paints, brushes, and canvas alone do not make a beautiful painting. An artist must have a plan, a vision of the ultimate creation. Similarly, your first task in a programming project is to determine what the outcome of your project will be. Unlike the world of fine arts, however, you do not usually make this decision. Your "customer," the computer user, does. Your role is to advise as to what expectations are reasonable. Together, you design the characteristics of the program's operation and output.

Once you define your goals, you must draw a map that shows how you plan to get from the project start to the project finish. This may be a flowchart that pictorially represents your plan, or it may be a pseudo program that contains brief English expressions of your ideas within a program structure. In any case, the document you create will guide you as your work progresses and later become one of the documents that illustrate what your program does.

This chapter discusses the frequently overlooked topic of program design and explains flowcharts and pseudocode. It uses the REM statement to provide the framework for a program's structure. The computer dating project illustrates programming from the planning stage through the writing of the program.

Flowcharts

A flowchart is a picture of the procedure for solving a problem. Special symbols and connecting lines illustrate each step in the solution and the order in which they should be taken. Drawing a flowchart forces you to carefully think a problem through. If you make a chart before you write a computer program, you are more likely to write an efficient program that takes into account all possibilities.

Flowcharts also enhance the usefulness of a computer program by making its logic clear. Both the International Organization for Standardization (ISO) and the American National Standards Institute (ANSI) have adopted several flowchart symbols. Thus, people not familiar with a program's computer language can understand how it works if the program is accompanied by a flowchart using these standard symbols.

The solution to any problem can be illustrated in a flowchart. A common problem and its solution are shown in Illustration 9.1. This flowchart is actually the result of using the standard symbols in connection with a few rules. The list of most frequently used symbols appears in Illustration 9.2. The flowchart rules are listed below:

1. Use straight lines that are vertical or horizontal.
2. Make all lines lead to a symbol.
3. Make sure that only one line leads to a symbol.
4. Make sure that lines do not cross one another; use connectors.
5. Use arrow marks on connecting lines when the flow is to the left or upward; otherwise arrows are not needed.
6. Include words like YES or NO at decision points to clarify when the flow should take a particular direction.
7. *Keep it simple.* Not every solution step is needed; chart only the ones that make it clear how the problem is being solved.

Read through the snowman flowchart (Illustration 9.1) again and notice how it exemplifies these flowchart rules.

Illustration 9.1 is a descriptive flowchart, one that includes explanatory text in the flowchart symbols. Computer programmers normally use symbolic flowcharts with brief symbols such as $X = X + 6$ within the flowchart symbols. They append descriptive comments on the margins with dashed lines. Illustration 9.3 is a symbolic flowchart. It charts the procedure for averaging scores for 20 students in a class where not all students took the same number of tests.

ILLUSTRATION 9.1

Building a snowman

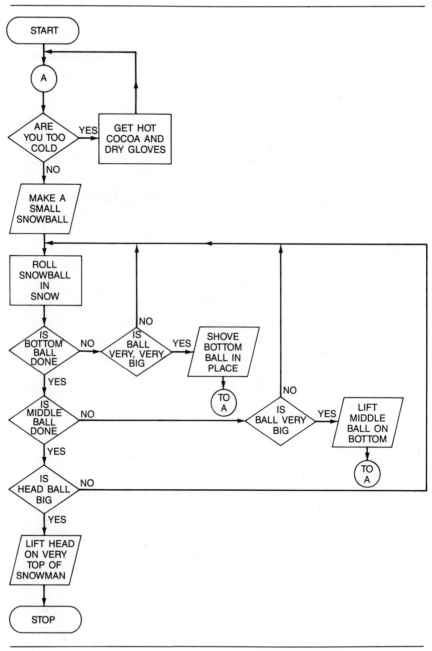

ILLUSTRATION 9.2

Flowchart symbols

Symbol	Description	Example
	Terminus: The start or any stopping point in the program	START
	Input/output: READ, INPUT, PRINT, operations as well as reading and writing disk or tape files	INPUT Y
	Decisions: Any operation that determines which one of two paths to follow	X = Y YES / NO
	Processing: Operations that change the value or form of information	X = X + 1
	Subroutine processing	X = X + 1 RETURN
	Data	DATA20,30,40
	Preparation: Set initial values, open files, set dimensions	DIM A(50)
	Connection: Exit to or entry from another part of chart	2
	Off page connection: Exit to another part of chart on separate page	4

ILLUSTRATION 9.3

Averaging a variable number of test scores for 20 students

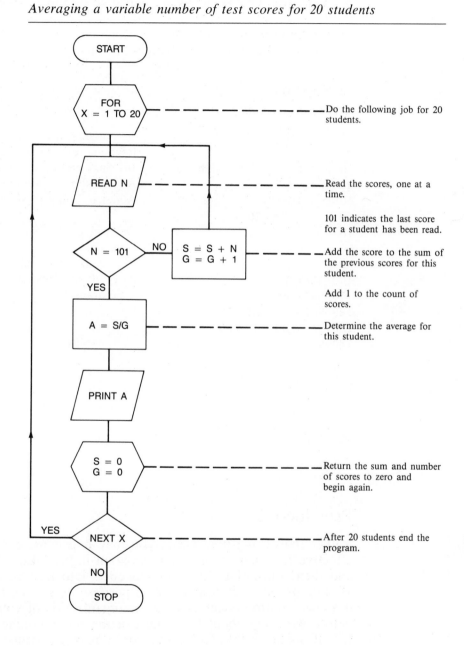

START

FOR
X = 1 TO 20 — — — — — — — — — — Do the following job for 20
students.

READ N — — — — — — — — — — — Read the scores, one at a
time.

101 indicates the last score
for a student has been read.

N = 101   NO   S = S + N
G = G + 1 — — — — — Add the score to the sum of
the previous scores for this
student.

YES

Add 1 to the count of
scores.

A = S/G — — — — — — — — — — Determine the average for
this student.

PRINT A

S = 0
G = 0 — — — — — — — — — — — Return the sum and number
of scores to zero and
begin again.

YES   NEXT X — — — — — — — — — After 20 students end the
program.

NO

STOP

Notice that not every step in the problem-solving process has been charted. GO TO ideas are indicated by the connecting lines. DATA statements are not included in the chart because their placement is not integral to the solution of the problem. Illustration 9.4 is a BASIC program derived from this symbolic flowchart.

ILLUSTRATION 9.4

Averaging a variable number of test scores for 20 students

10 FOR X = 1 TO 20	20 students in the class.
20 READ N	Read scores one at a time.
30 IF N = 101 THEN 70	101 flags end of student's scores.
40 S = S+N	Add to sum of previous scores.
50 G = G+1	Add 1 to count of scores.
60 GO TO 20	
70 A = S/G	Determine this student's average.
80 PRINT A	Print the average.
90 S,G = 0	Reinitialize the counters.
100 NEXT X	After 20 students, stop the
110 DATA 89, 87, 86, 101	program.
120 DATA 88, 56, 77, 101	
130 DATA 90, 91, 89, 88, 101	
140 and so on	
150 with data for	
160 20 students	

```
.
.
.
999 END
```

Pseudocode

Rather than using flowcharts, you may find it more natural and effective to begin writing your program in brief English phrases and then translating this "pseudocode" into true BASIC code. Writing pseudocode has the same purpose as writing flowcharts: it allows you to concentrate on the organization of your program before worrying about the details of the programming language. BASIC makes it easy for you to work this way because it includes the REM, or remark, statement which stores programmer's notes.

The REM Statement

REM statements appear when you list your program, but they are ignored when the program runs (Illustration 9.5):

ILLUSTRATION 9.5

```
100 REM**** THIS IS THE JOURNEY OF LIFE ****
110 PRINT " THE SEASONS ARE THE AGES "
120 REM **** THIS IS THE SEASON OF JOY ****
130 PRINT " THE EARTH IS GREEN "
140 REM **** THIS IS THE SEASON OF LABOR ****
150 PRINT " THE LEAVES ARE FALLING "
160 REM **** THIS IS THE SEASON OF HOPE ****
170 PRINT " THE SNOW IS MELTING "
180 REM **** THIS IS THE TIME OF TRIUMPH ****
190 PRINT " EVERYONE SMILES "
200 END

RUN

THE SEASONS ARE THE AGES
THE EARTH IS GREEN
THE LEAVES ARE FALLING
THE SNOW IS MELTING
EVERYONE SMILES
```

Usually, REM statements are less dramatic. They often incorporate within the body of the program the programmer's name, the version of BASIC being used, and the program's completion date. They are also used as headings to remind you and others what each section of the program does.

Structuring a program with REM statements

If you use REM statements as headings, you can set out the structure of your program before you fill in the details. Write the REM statements first. Use one for each important segment of your program. For example, use REM for the pseudocode of a project to calculate gas mileage:

```
10 REM INPUT THE DISTANCE TRAVELED ON 20 GALLONS OF GAS
20 REM CALCULATE THE MILES PER GALLON
30 REM PRINT OUT THE RESULTS
40 END
```

The REM statements become the main routine of your program. Flesh out the details in distinct program modules and append them to the main routine as they are needed. Ultimately, you will have a clearly structured program driven by GO SUB statements (Illustration 9.6).

ILLUSTRATION 9.6

A structured program

```
10 REM INPUT THE DISTANCE TRAVELED ON 20 GALLONS OF GAS
12 GO SUB 100
20 REM CALCULATE THE MILES PER GALLON
22 GO SUB 200
30 REM PRINT OUT THE RESULTS
32 GO SUB 300
40 STOP
100 INPUT "ENTER THE DISTANCE TRAVELED";D
110 RETURN
200 M = D/20
210 RETURN
300 PRINT "YOUR CAR GETS";M;"MILES PER GALLON"
310 RETURN
400 END

RUN

ENTER THE DISTANCE TRAVELED? 500
YOUR CAR GETS 25 MILES PER GALLON
```

Programming in this fashion has the obvious disadvantage that it requires many more lines of code than are actually needed to solve the programming problem. REM statements slow down program execution even though they are ignored as the program runs. The important advantage is that the logic of your solution is crystal clear. Your program works well because each of the modules has been written and tested before it becomes part of the program. Many programmers achieve the best of all worlds by storing a well-documented version of a program in their files and actually running a ''stripped-down'' version with no REM statements.

The real place for pseudocode and structured programming is in bigger projects. The section on the Computer Dating Project puts you in the programmer's seat and takes you through the project's planning, design, and execution. Once you've read the section, include the program in your own program library. You will discover that you and your computer become very popular with some of your friends and not so popular with others.

The STOP Statement and the CONT Command

The STOP statement in line 40 of Illustration 9.6 separates the main routine from the subroutines by causing the program to halt execution. The computer prints the message:

```
BREAK IN 40
```

This tells the line number of the STOP statement. If you were searching for a problem, the STOP statement would be very helpful. Now, you could enter "direct mode commands" (BASIC statements without line numbers) to find out if your program has done what you expected. Type:

```
PRINT D
```

and the computer will print the current value of the variable, D. Typing:

```
GO TO 10
```

causes the computer to RUN the program beginning at line 10 or whatever line you indicate. You can even change the value of a variable by entering a LET statement:

```
D = 5
```

Finally, when you are ready to see what your program will do next, enter:

```
CONT
```

Your program will continue from the line following the STOP statement that caused the halt. STOP and CONT are powerful program development tools. Insert STOP statements throughout your program as you work. Remove them when everything is working as you intend.

The Computer Dating Project

The Social Committee has the problem of gracefully integrating new members into the group. The computer, with its thick skin, is elected to handle the delicate task of "breaking the ice" and deciding on partners for the first dance. As the programmer, you are called in to write the program that will create the pairs.

Together, you and the Committee boldly decide to follow the theory that opposites attract. All members will receive a questionnaire like the one in Illustration 9.7, and their answers will be entered into the computer. Your program will evaluate all of the responses and assign a "coefficient of compatibility" between each male and each female. Then it will search the coefficients to find the man and woman with the greatest differences (the highest coefficient) and declare them to be the first pair. These two will be eliminated from further consideration, and the next most different couple will be selected. Eventually, all of the respondents will be paired.

ILLUSTRATION 9.7

Computer dating questionnaire

Name __*Amy Bryan*__   Sex __*F*__

I. Life-style Emphasis:
   1. What percent of your time do you devote to the pursuit of material goods (e.g., grades, status, money)? __*20*__

   2. What percent of your time is devoted to personal relations? __*80*__

   (These two percents must add up to 100%.)

II. Pursuit of Material Goods:
   Rate your level of preference for the following activities using the following scale: 1—strong preference . . . 9—no liking.
   3. Desk work __*1*__ 4. Lab work __*3*__ 5. Writing __*5*__
   6. Walking in the woods __*3*__ 7. Playing on a team __*3*__

III. Personal Relations:
   Answer these questions using the following values:
      1—Definitely yes   3—Don't care   9—Definitely no
      8. My date must be very physically attractive. __*9*__

   9. Other people's opinions of me matter a great deal. __*3*__

   10. It is perfectly OK to kiss on the first date. __*1*__

   11. A lasting, meaningful relationship is better than a short, intense one. __*9*__

   12. A date is primarily for having a good time, not necessarily for getting to know one another. __*3*__

Of course, the final couples will have fewer differences than the first ones and, according to the theory, may not be very compatible at all. Nevertheless, the Committee wishes to use all of the pairs because its real purpose is to have everyone meet someone. The ice will be broken in one way or another!

The only restriction is that there must be an equal number of men and women, so a way must be found to eliminate extras. The Committee decides that first-come, first-served is as good a basis as any, and agrees to use questionnaires in the order that they are received.

Notice that the Committee's questionnaire first asks what percent of a person's life is devoted to the pursuit of material goods and what percent to personal relations. These percents will be applied as weighting factors to the remaining questions, which are grouped as "material goods" questions and "personal relationship" ones.

In order to speed the data entry process, each answer to these remaining questions will be a number from 1 to 9 that indicates how strongly one favors the statement. Thus, the answers given to the questions in Illustration 9.7 will be entered as:

20,80,1,3,5,3,3,9,3,1,9,3

The printout that the Committee wishes is simply a list of the pairs:

Ideal Partners
Samantha Wilder and Lindsay Hurdle
Bertha Blue and George Street

.
.
.

etc.

Having defined your goals, your meeting with the Committee ends. It is time to head for the drawing board to work out the pseudocode of your program. Illustration 9.8 is an example of such a code. It forms the basis for the computer dating program of Illustration 9.9.

This dating program accepts the participants' names and responses from disk files. In a project such as this one where large amounts of data are likely to be required, it is a good idea to separate the data entry and the data processing procedures. By using files, you can take time to enter, review, and correct your data in one program. When the data are perfect, you can set in motion another processing program. Because you know that the data are correct, you can have confidence in the processing results. Lines 100 to 190 in Illustration 9.9 read the data files. Don't be concerned if you do not understand them now. Chapters 12, 13 and 14 explain data file processing in detail.

The Appendix, Operating Instructions for the Dating Program, includes a group of companion programs that make it easy to store, correct, and use the dating program and its data. You may want to set up a separate disk that holds only the main program and these auxiliary ones.

The error-handling routine in lines 400 through 500 traps the Out-of-paper error that occurs if the printer is not turned on. Lines 442 and 443 delay processing to give time for getting the printer ready.

ILLUSTRATION 9.8

Pseudocode for the computer dating program

```
10 REM IDENTIFICATION

20 REM SET UP ERROR TRAP
```

```
30 REM HOW MANY PAIRS? HOW MANY QUESTIONS?

40 REM SET DIMENSIONS
42 REM F$(no. of females), F(no. of females, no. of questions)
44 REM M$(no. of males), M(no. of males, no. of questions)
46 REM S(no. of females, no. of males)

50 REM INPUT NAMES AND RESPONSES
52 GO SUB 100

60 REM CALCULATE DIFFERENCES AND CREATE "COEFFICIENTS OF COMPATIBILITY"
62 GO SUB 200

70 REM SEARCH COEFFICIENTS FOR BEST MATCHES
72 GO SUB 300

80 STOP

100 REM INPUT FEMALE NAMES AND RESPONSES
150 REM INPUT MALE NAMES AND RESPONSES
190 RETURN

200 REM CLEAR SCREEN
210 REM COMPARE EACH MALE WITH EACH FEMALE:
220 REM CALCULATE WEIGHT FACTORS
230 REM COMPARE AND WEIGH "MATERIAL WORLD" RESPONSES
240 REM COMPARE AND WEIGH PERSONAL RELATIONS RESPONSES
250 REM IF THIS COEFFICIENT IS HIGHEST SO FAR, STORE IT IN H
260 REM STORE COEFFICIENT FOR THIS PAIR IN S( , )
270 REM RETURN

300 REM PRINT RESULTS
310 REM FIND PAIR WITH HIGHEST COEFFICIENT
320 REM ELIMINATE CHOSEN PAIR—SET THEIR COEFFICIENTS TO -1
330 REM PRINT NAMES OF CHOSEN PAIR
340 REM RETURN

400 REM IF PRINTER IS NOT ON SEND A REMINDER
410 REM RETURN ALL OTHER ERRORS TO NORMAL ERROR HANDLER

500 END
```

ILLUSTRATION 9.9

Computer dating program

```
10 REM THE COMPUTER DATING PROGRAM
11 REM WRITTEN BY HARRIET MORRILL
12 REM JULY 1983
13 REM WESLEYAN UNIVERSITY
14 REM MIDDLETOWN CT
15 REM IBM PC DISK BASIC 1.1
20 ON ERROR GOTO 400
30 INPUT"HOW MANY PAIRS";Z
32 INPUT"HOW MANY QUESTIONS";Q
40 DIM F$(Z),F(Z,Q),M$(Z),M(Z,Q),S(Z,Z)
50 REM INPUT NAMES AND RESPONSES
52 GOSUB 100
60 REM CALCULATE DIFFERENCES AND CREATE "COEFFICIENTS OF COMPATIBILITY"
62 GOSUB 200
70 REM SEARCH COEFFICIENTS FOR BEST MATCHES
72 GOSUB 300
75 REM END THE PROGRAM
80 GOTO 500
100 REM INPUT FEMALES' NAMES AND RESPONSES
104 OPEN "FEMALES" AS 1
106 FOR X = 1 TO Z
107     GET #1
108     FIELD 1, 30 AS N$, 2*Q AS D$
110     F$(X)=N$
112     FOR Y = 1 TO Q
114             FIELD 1, 30 AS N$,(Y-1)*2 AS D$, 2 AS R$
116             F(X,Y)=CVI(R$)
118     NEXT Y
120 NEXT X
130 CLOSE 1
150 REM INPUT MALES' NAMES AND RESPONSES
152 OPEN "MALES" AS 1
155 FOR X = 1 TO Z
157     GET #1
158     FIELD 1, 30 AS N$,2*Q AS D$
160     M$(X)=N$
165     FOR Y = 1 TO Q
170             FIELD 1, 30 AS N$,(Y-1)*2 AS D$,2 AS R$
172             M(X,Y)=CVI(R$)
174     NEXT Y
```

```
180 NEXT X
185 CLOSE 1
190 RETURN
200 REM CLEAR SCREEN
202 CLS
203 PRINT TAB(12),"DATING MAGIC"
204 PRINT TAB(12),"IN PROCESS ..."
206 PRINT:PRINT:PRINT:PRINT
208 H = 0: K = 100
210 REM COMPARE EACH MALE WITH EACH FEMALE
212 FOR R = 1 TO Z
214     FOR W = 1 TO Z
217             C = 0
220 REM CALCULATE WEIGHTING FACTORS
222             P1 = (F(R,1)+M(W,1))/K
224             P2 = (F(R,2)+M(W,2))/K
230 REM COMPARE AND WEIGH "MATERIAL WORLD" RESPONSES
232             FOR E = 3 TO INT(Q/2)
234                     C =C+ABS(INT((F(R,E)-M(W,E))*P1))
236             NEXT E
240 REM COMPARE AND WEIGH PERSONAL RELATIONS RESPONSES
242             FOR E = INT(Q/2) + 1 TO Q
244                     C=C+ABS(INT((F(R,E)-M(W,E))*P2))
246             NEXT E
250 REM IS THIS COEFFICIENT THE HIGHEST? IF SO,STORE IN H
252             IF C < H THEN 260
254             H=C
260 REM STORE COEFFICIENT FOR THIS PAIR IN S( , )
262             S(R,W) = C
266     NEXT W
268 NEXT R
270 RETURN
300 REM PRINT RESULTS
304 LPRINT "THE IDEAL PARTNERS"
306 PRINT:PRINT
310 REM FIND PAIRS WITH HIGHEST COEFFICIENT IN S( , )
312 FOR J = H TO 0 Step = 1
314     FOR W = 1 TO Z
316             FOR E = 1 TO Z
318                     IF S(W,E) <>J THEN 334
320 REM ELIMINATE CHOSEN PAIR - SET THEIR COEFFICIENT TO -1
322                     FOR T = 1 TO Z
324                             S(W,T) = -1
```

```
326                         S(T,E) = -1
328                    NEXT T
329                    Z9 = Z9 +1
330 REM PRINT NAMES OF CHOSEN PAIR
332             LPRINT F$(W);" and ";M$(E):PRINT
333             IF Z9 = Z THEN 340
334             NEXT E
336      NEXT W
338 NEXT J
340 RETURN
400 REM IF PRINTER IS NOT ON SEND A REMINDER
410 IF ERR <> 27 THEN ON ERROR GOTO 0
415 CLS
420 PRINT "TURN ON PRINTER "
442 FOR X = 1 TO 5000
443 NEXT
445 CLS
450 RESUME 300
500 END
```

Problems

1. Draw the flowchart for the familiar problem of selecting and watching a prime-time TV show. Remember that commercials usually signal the end of the show or time to get a quick snack.

2. Draw the flowchart for a 20-question foreign language drill. Use READ and DATA for the quiz information and keep track of the number of correct answers given. If an answer is incorrect, give the student two more tries to get it right. At the end of the quiz, print out the student's score.

3. Carry on with your study of the remaining chapters. Write pseudocode as you develop solutions to the programming problems you are asked to do. Hand in the pseudocode along with your computer programs.

Chapter 10

Graphics and Color

Before the advent of colorful computer graphics, reading computer results was tedious. Information highlights were buried among information details. Computer games were more like computer work.

"Lunar Lander" was a popular early computer game. In those days the players sat at black and white screens watching columns of numbers that represented the changing altitude and speed of their landing craft. By typing commands they tried to negotiate a safe, soft landing on the moon. If they failed, there appeared on the screen a phrase such as SURFACE IMPACT . . . SHIP DE-STROYED . . . NO SURVIVORS. Or, perhaps, if they were lucky they saw: ALTITUDE 0 . . . LANDING SUCCESSFUL. "Computer Golf" was an exercise in speed reading. Long paragraphs describing the course ("There is a sand trap on your left and a tree to the right. The fairway slopes at an angle of 18 degrees. . . .") led to the final question: "Which club do you choose?" After each "shot" another description appeared, so that completing a computer round of golf was nearly as time-consuming as the real game.

Serious computer information was equally dry. An analysis of your mortgage payments would be a list of dates and figures. Today, however, on the IBM personal computer even such dreary news as how much you still owe can be dramatically clear if not actually fun to see.

The impact of the microcomputer revolution on this aspect of computing has been as dramatic and as important as its effect on reducing computing costs and increasing computing capacity. The BASIC language now includes statements that produce colorful displays, and you can use them in a program in the same fashion as the usual BASIC statements. These graphic statements are not only fun to use but they also greatly enhance the effectiveness of the usual data processing and calculating computer functions. They permit you to present otherwise tedious results in a vivid and clear manner.

If you have a color/graphics adapter on the IBM personal computer, you can choose between medium-resolution displays that allow 16 colors or high-resolution displays with only black and white color but much greater detail. This chapter explains the fundamental simple graphics statements that are good tools for creating "still life" screen displays. These are the SCREEN, PSET, PRESET, LINE, CIRCLE and PAINT statements. Chapter 11 explains the more complex and powerful graphics statements that make it easy to create animated displays.

Choosing the Display Mode

When it comes to doing output, the computer needs to know which display mode you will be working in; text, medium-resolution graphics, or high-resolution graphics. In text mode, the computer assumes that you will create displays and printed results with the PRINT and LPRINT statements; it thinks of the screen as having 25 lines for printing, with up to 80 character positions on each line.

In either of the graphics modes, the computer views the screen as a grid of picture elements, or PELs. You create graphics displays by telling the computer to light up or turn off various PELs. Lighting a shape of PELs, turning it off, and relighting the same configuration in a different location creates the illusion of movement.

Both the medium- and the high-resolution screens have 200 rows of PELs numbered from 0 at the top of the screen to 199 at the bottom. The medium-resolution screen has 320 PELs in a row, with PEL 0 on the left and number 319 on the far right. Each row of the high-resolution display has 640 PELs ranging from 0 on the left to 639 on the right.

Illustration 10.1 depicts the location of the PEL at position (3,20). The PEL is described by first giving the horizontal location

ILLUSTRATION 10.1

Locating the PEL at position (3,20)

```
                         Positions
                  0  1  2  3  4  5  6  7  8  . . .
                 ─────────────────────────────────
           0
           1
           2
           3
  Rows     4
           5
           ⋮
          20              ° (3,20)
           ⋮
         199
                 ─────────────────────────────────
```

and then its vertical, or row designation. The PEL at (3,20) is 4 positions across from the left of the screen and 21 positions down from the top.

Graphics statements will not work in the text mode, but the text output statements like PRINT and LPRINT will work in the graphics modes. PRINT in the medium resolution permits 40 characters in a line and allows 25 lines. PRINT in the high resolution uses 80 characters for a line and also allows 25 lines.

When you are in graphics modes, line 25 makes a good display label because you can PRINT to it and it will not scroll as other print lines do. Before you can use it, you must turn off the special function key prompts that usually appear on this line. Begin your program with a statement that includes the command:

```
50 KEY OFF
```

The SCREEN Statement

The SCREEN statement tells the computer which mode of display will be in effect for the program statements that follow. The statement

```
10 SCREEN 1,0
```

sets the display for medium resolution (1) and no color (0). Illustration 10.2 shows all of the available combinations of mode and color.

ILLUSTRATION 10.2

Mode and color combinations in the SCREEN statement

Statement	Mode/Color
10 SCREEN 0,0	Text mode/no color
10 SCREEN 0,1	Text mode/with color
10 SCREEN 1,0	Medium Resolution/with color
10 SCREEN 1,1	Medium Resolution/no color
10 SCREEN 2	High Resolution/no color

Using SCREEN to Store Pages of Text Displays

The graphics capabilities require that a large portion of RAM serve as a staging area, or buffer, for the displays prior to being sent to the screen. The text mode takes advantage of the fact that it does not need all of this large I/O buffer in setting up each character display. Text mode divides the I/O buffer into eight pages (0 through 7) to hold 40-character-wide displays or four pages (0 to 3) of 80-character-wide displays. You can use the SCREEN statement to choose, first, which of the text mode pages you want to display and, second, which one you want to write in. They need not be the same page.

```
10 SCREEN 0,1,1,2
```

tells the computer to consider the display to be text mode (0) with color on (1). Page one (1) of the I/O buffer is the active page and all PRINT statement output will be directed there. Page two (2) of the display buffer will be the one shown on the screen.

The COLOR Statement

Medium-resolution color displays on the IBM personal computer are impressive! Once you've created one you'll most likely find yourself trying to work them into the most mundane projects.

The COLOR statement sets up a background color and a selection (palette) of three colors that you can use for lines and shapes. Medium resolution has no border color. High resolution has no color at all.

The possible background colors are the 16 colors listed in Chapter 1, Illustration 1.4. There are two palettes to choose from. Illustration 10.3 shows the colors available on each palette.

ILLUSTRATION 10.3

The colors in palettes 0 and 1

Color number	Color	Color number	Color
Palette 0		Palette 1	
1	green	1	cyan
2	red	2	magenta
3	brown	3	white

The colors from Palette 0 on a background of light blue make beautiful displays. To enter medium-resolution graphics and select these colors, begin your program with:

```
10 SCREEN 1,0
20 COLOR 9,0
```

Nine in the COLOR statement selects the background of light blue. Zero selects the palette. Later graphics statements will require that you choose one of the color numbers from Palette 0.

The PSET and PRESET Statements

These statements perform the fundamental graphics display task of setting individual PELs on and off. Fortunately, IBM personal computer BASIC has other graphics statements that allow you to describe large areas of the screen at once so that you need not always work with just one PEL at a time.

Light a PEL with the PSET(,) statement that includes its horizontal and vertical coordinates.

```
10 SCREEN 1,0
20 COLOR 9,0
30 PSET (160,100),2
```

The PSET statement in line 30 puts a tiny red dot in the center of the medium-resolution screen. It lights the PEL that is in position 160 over from the left margin and 101 rows down from the top. The 2 represents red, the second color in Palette 0. This is the palette chosen by the COLOR statement in line 20.

Either PSET (,),0 or PRESET (,) erase a PEL by lighting it in the background color. (Aside from this difference, PSET (,) and PRESET (,) are exactly the same.) Thus, adding the line:

```
40 PSET(160,100),0
```

makes the red dot disappear.

Illustration 10.4 draws a red line by lighting a series of the PELs. All of the PELs from left to right (0 to 319) along row 100 are lit as the FOR . . . NEXT loop proceeds.

ILLUSTRATION 10.4

Drawing a line with PSET (,)

```
10 CLS
20 SCREEN 1,0
30 COLOR 9,0
40 FOR X = 0 TO 319
50     PSET (X,100),2
60 NEXT X
70 END


RUN
```

Make a cross design by lighting PELs down a column of the medium-resolution display grid as well:

ILLUSTRATION 10.5

Using PSET (,) to draw crossed lines

```
10 CLS
20 SCREEN 1,0
30 COLOR 9,0
40 FOR X = 0 TO 319
50     PSET (X,100),2
60 NEXT X
70 FOR Y = 0 TO 199
80     PSET (160,Y),2
90 NEXT Y
100 END
```

Create flickers by randomly PSETting a PEL in a palette color and then PSETting the same PEL in the background color. Illustration 10.6 uses the random number function to choose a random number in the range of 0 to 319. This becomes the horizontal position; another number in the range of 0 to 199 becomes the row location. When these randomly selected numbers become coordinates in the PSET(,) statement, they light up PELs at unpredictable points on the screen.

ILLUSTRATION 10.6

Creating flickers with PSET (,)

```
10 RANDOMIZE 567
20 SCREEN 1,0
30 CLS
40 COLOR 9,0
50 FOR X = 1 to 500
60     H = INT(RND*319)
70     V = INT(RND*199)
80     PSET (H,V),2
85     PSET (H+1,V+1),2
90     PSET (H,V),0
95     PSET (H+1,V+1),0
100 NEXT X
110 END
```

Notice that Illustration 10.6 sets two adjacent PELs to color 2 (red). Then, in lines 90 and 95 PSET (,) turns them off with color 0 (background). PELs are so tiny that lighting one alone is hardly noticeable. Lighting two at a time is often more effective. Lines 85 and 95 also show that you can use variables and expressions as well as constants to define the location of a PEL.

The LINE Statement

ILLUSTRATION 10.7

Using LINE to draw crossed lines

```
10 SCREEN 1,0
20 COLOR 9,0
30 LINE (0,100) -(319,100),2
40 LINE (160,0) -(160,199),2
50 END
```

Illustration 10.7 produces the same red cross as Illustration 10.5, but it does so with many fewer program statements. The LINE statement makes it possible to produce a line by simply describing its beginning and ending PELs. In line 30, where the horizontal values change from 0 to 319, it draws the line across row 100. In line 40, where the vertical values change, it draws a line down the PELs in column 160. Both LINE statements include the palette color number 2 for red. If you do not specify a color, the LINE statement uses number 3 of the current palette.

As your program runs, you can pick up drawing where you left off with a LINE statement that has coordinates preceded by a minus sign. If the statement

```
45 LINE -(319,0)
```

were added to Illustration 10.7, a diagonal line would appear running from the last PEL lighted in line 40 (160,199), to the upper right-hand corner of the screen (319,0). Such drawing need not be continuous; your program can do other processing and then return to the screen. The computer will not forget where drawing left off.

You can also draw rectangles with the LINE statement. If you do, the two sets of coordinates represent: first, the lower leftmost PEL; then, the opposite PEL, the one in the upper rightmost corner. You must also add the B box parameter so that the computer knows not to just draw a line between these points. If you also specify a palette color number and the F, fill, parameter, the computer will color the box.

```
10 LINE (80,175) -(100,25),2,BF
```

produces a red box similar to the one in Illustration 10.8.

ILLUSTRATION 10.8

A rectangle produced by the LINE statement

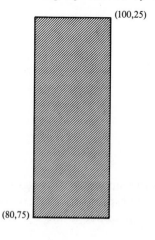

   Illustration 10.9 is a BASIC program that uses a brightly colored bar graph for illustrating how much of the monthly mortgage payment actually goes towards reducing the amount owed and how much goes to the money lender as interest. The beginning lines calculate, for any one month, the division of the monthly payment between interest and principal. Lines 57 through 88 set up screen labels.

   The heart of the program is in lines 130 and 140. These create a bar graph with narrow rectangles representing the portions of the monthly payment. Line 130 draws a rectangle whose height illustrates the dollars devoted to interest (IPAY). It lies between the 90th and 100th column of PELs and rests along the 189th row. It reaches up to the row that is IPAY number of PELs above the 189th row (closer to row zero: 189 - IPAY). Line 140 draws another bar whose height illustrates the dollars devoted to reducing the principal. It lies between column 200 and 210 and reaches from row 189 to the row of PELs, that is, RDCE PELs above it.

ILLUSTRATION 10.9

Using LINE to create a bar graph

```
1 REM SET UP GRAPHICS SCREEN & COLOR
2 SCREEN 1,0
3 COLOR 9,0
4 CLS
5 INPUT "ENTER THE PAYMENT MONTH";MNTH
10 READ PRINC,RATE,PAYMNT
11 REM CALCULATE PAYMENT AMOUNTS
12 FOR X = 1 TO MNTH
14     IPAY = INT(PRINC*RATE)
15     RDCE = INT(PAYMENT-IPAY)
16     PRINC = PRINC-RDCE
50 NEXT X
55 CLS
57 REM DRAW GRAPH LABELS
60 LOCATE 25,7
65 PRINT "DIVISION OF PAYMENT NO.";MNTH
66 LOCATE 3,3
67 PRINT "$500"
68 LOCATE 14,3
69 PRINT "250"
75 LOCATE 3,9
76 PRINT "INTEREST"
80 LOCATE 3,22
85 PRINT "PRINCIPAL"
```

```
88 REM SCALE AMOUNTS TO FIT THE GRAPH
90 IPAY = IPAY/3
95 RDCE = RDCE/3
99 REM DISPLAY AMOUNTS IN BAR GRAPH
125 LINE (50,17) -(50,191)
130 LINE (90,189) -(100,(189-IPAY)),,BF
140 LINE (200,189) -(210,(189-RDCE)),,BF
150 LINE (50,191) -(250,191)
900 DATA 25000,.01,300
999 END
```

The CIRCLE Statement

The CIRCLE statement makes it easy to draw circles, arcs, pie slices, and ellipses of all sorts. For example:

```
10 CIRCLE(160,100),80
```

draws a circle with its center at position 160,100 and a radius of 80 PELs, and

```
10 CIRCLE(160,100),80,2
```

draws the same circle in color number 2 of your chosen palette.

The computer thinks of the circle as geometry students do: divided into angles ranging from 0 to $\pi/2$ to π to $3\pi/2$ and back to 2π radians:

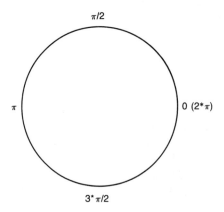

If you wish to draw an arc, you need to refer to points on the circle. To do this, assign the value of π, 3.141593, to a variable in a LET statement and use the variable when referring to the starting and end positions of the arc. These positions are given as additional parameters in the CIRCLE statement:

```
10 PI = 3.141593
20 CIRCLE (160,100),80,2,(2*PI),(PI/2)
```

start end

```
RUN
```

As the RUN indicates, these statements produce an arc that reaches from 2*PI (or 0) to position PI/2 on the circumference of the circle with the center at position 160,100 and a radius of 80 PELs.

If you put a minus sign before the start and end points, you get a slice of pie:

```
10 PI = 3.141593
20 CIRCLE (160,100),80,2,-2*PI,-PI/2
```

```
RUN
```

The computer draws the arc you have described and connects its end positions to the center with straight lines.

Illustration 10.10 adds a section to the mortgage payment program in Illustration 10.9 to create a colorful pie chart showing the percentage of the monthly payment going to interest and the percentage going to reduce the amount owed. Line 205 (which defines PI as π) is easy to forget, but essential if you wish to refer to the angles of a circle. Line 210 draws an outline of the pie chart: the circle centered at 160,100 with a radius of 80 PELs. Line 240 draws the portion of the circle representing the percentage of the payment that is interest (I). The remaining wedge represents the reduction in principal (RDCE). The PAINT statements that follow fill each wedge with a different color, making it easy to see which portion of the entire circle each wedge represents.

ILLUSTRATION 10.10

Using CIRCLE to create a pie chart

```
1 REM SET UP GRAPHICS SCREEN & COLOR
2 SCREEN 1,0
3 COLOR 9,0
4 CLS
5 INPUT "ENTER THE PAYMENT MONTH";MNTH
10 READ PRINC,RATE,PAYMNT
11 REM CALCULATE PAYMENT AMOUNTS
12 FOR X = 1 TO MNTH
14    IPAY = INT(PRINC*RATE)
15    RDCE = INT(PAYMNT-IPAY)
16    PRINC = PRINC-RDCE
50 NEXT X
55 CLS
57 REM DRAW GRAPH LABELS
60 LOCATE 25,7
65 PRINT "DIVISION OF PAYMENT NO.";MNTH
66 LOCATE 3,3
67 PRINT "500$"
68 LOCATE 14,3
69 PRINT "250"
75 LOCATE 3,9
76 PRINT "INTEREST"
80 LOCATE 3,22
85 PRINT "PRINCIPAL"
88 REM SCALE AMOUNTS TO FIT THE GRAPH
90 IPAY = IPAY/3
95 RDCE = RDCE/3
99 REM DISPLAY AMOUNTS IN BAR GRAPH
125 LINE (50,17) -(50,191)
130 LINE (90,189) -(100,(189-IPAY)),,BF
140 LINE (200,189) -(210,(189-RDCE)),,BF
150 LINE (50,191) -(250,191)
155 REM HOLD GRAPH ON SCREEN
160 FOR X = 1 TO 5000
170 NEXT X
200 REM SHOW PERCENTAGES IN A PIE CHART
201 CLS
205 PI = 3.141593
210 CIRCLE (160,100),80,3
220 I = IPAY/(PAYMNT/3)
222 LOCATE 12,1
```

```
224 PRINT "INTEREST"
226 PRINT INT(I*100);"%"
230 R=RDCE/(PAYMNT/3)
232 LOCATE 12,32
234 PRINT "PRINCIPAL"
235 LOCATE 13,34
236 PRINT "INT(R*100);"%"
240 CIRCLE (160,100),80,3,-2*PI,-I*(2*PI)
245 PAINT (158,98),1,3
248 PAINT (162,102),2,3
250 LOCATE 25,9
260 PRINT "PERCENT OF MONTHLY PAYMENT#";MNTH
900 DATA 25000,.01,300
999 END
```

Create an egg shape by adding an arithmetic expression as the final parameter of a CIRCLE statement. If the value of the expression is less than 1, the egg will lie on its side. If it is greater than 1, the egg will stand up:

```
10 CIRCLE (160,100),80,3, , ,3/4
```

RUN

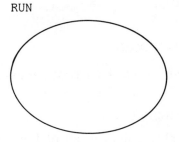

```
10 CIRCLE (160,100),80, , ,2/1
```

RUN

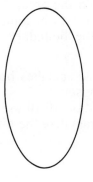

All of the parameters of the CIRCLE statement are positional, and except for the center and the radius, they are optional. They must occur in this order: center, radius, color, start point, end point, and aspect. They must be separated by commas. If you omit a parameter, you must still indicate its position by inserting the comma that usually separates it from the next parameter. The last parameter you give need not be followed by a comma.

Once the CIRCLE statement executes, the computer considers that the center is the "last point referenced." This is important if you later execute a graphics statement that continues from the "last point referenced." This later statement will begin its work at the center of your circle. Illustration 10.11 takes advantage of this to draw a red lollipop on a yellow stick.

ILLUSTRATION 10.11

Continuing from the last point referenced

```
5 PI = 3.141593
10 SCREEN 1,0
20 COLOR 9,0
22 CIRCLE (160,100),60,2
25 LINE -(160,199)
```

The PAINT Statement

Enter Illustration 10.11 into your IBM personal computer and add the statement:

```
30 PAINT (162,98),2,2
```

The computer quickly colors in all of the lollipop and makes it bright red. The PAINT statement is a wonderful statement that allows you to color large areas of the screen by:

1. specifying any point within the area.
2. noting the color you want it to become.
3. specifying the color of the boundary you do not wish to cross.

The PAINT statement in line 30 specifies both colors as number 2, the second in the palette chosen.

Lines 245 and 248 in Illustration 10.10 use PAINT to fill in the portions of the pie chart and dramatize the difference between the two.

```
245 PAINT (158,98),1,3
```

points to a PEL within the interest portion of the pie and paints it color number 1, green, up to the border of the circle, color number 3, brown.

```
248 PAINT (162,102),2,3
```

points to a PEL within the principal portion of the pie and paints it color number 2, red, up to the border of the circle, color number 3.

Take a few minutes to enter Illustration 10.10 into your IBM personal computer. Run it, and consider how much more effective is the graphic presentation of the report, as compared with an early computer printout that would have been a table of dates and numbers in black and white.

The LOCATE Statement for Cursor Design

Even though the blinking cursor appears to be a thin blinking line, the computer considers it to be a rectangle of PELs like the one in Illustration 10.12.

ILLUSTRATION 10.12

The computer's view of the cursor (greatly enlarged)

```
1 . . . . . . . . . . . . . . . . . . . . . .
2 . . . . . . . . . . . . . . . . . . . . . .
3 . . . . . . . . . . . . . . . . . . . . . .
4 . . . . . . . . . . . . . . . . . . . . . .
5 . . . . . . . . . . . . . . . . . . . . . .
6 . . . . . . . . . . . . . . . . . . . . . .
7 . . . . . . . . . . . . . . . . . . . . . .
```

Usually, row 7 is lit, but the LOCATE statement allows you to determine whether or not it will be visible as it races across the screen. Adding a 0 makes it disappear; a 1 keeps the cursor visible.

```
10 LOCATE 12,40,0
```

In this line 10, the third parameter, 0, turns the cursor off during its move to the twelfth row and position 40.

```
10 LOCATE 12,40,1
```

Here, the third parameter, 1, keeps the cursor on.

LOCATE also allows you to specify which rows of cursor PELs will be visible. After the third parameter, which turns the cursor on, add the starting row and the ending row.

```
10 LOCATE 12,40,1,1,7
```

sends the largest cursor possible with all seven rows of PELs lit, to row 12, position 40.

```
LOCATE 12,40,1,1,3
```

sends a cursor with its three top rows visible, a shorter rectangle, to the middle screen position.

Chapter 11

Animation, Music, and Unusual Input

This chapter continues the discussion of BASIC language tools for creating interesting computer displays. It presents the DRAW, GET, PUT, BEEP, SOUND and PLAY statements that allow animation and music. DRAW and PLAY are powerful statements that are really mini-languages within the BASIC language.

Chapter 11 ends by touching upon what may be the next frontier of computer technology: the realm of the computer user's experience. The INPUT statement and the Enter Key may become obsolete as users communicate their reactions to the computer with a gesture or a wink. The ability to understand such human responses has not yet been incorporated into BASIC, but the language does enable the user to work with interesting input devices such as light pens and joysticks. This chapter shows how the INKEY$ function and the ON PEN GO SUB and ON STRIG GO SUB statements make it possible to program interesting input routines.

The DRAW Statement

All of the special DRAW statement commands are listed in Illustration 11.1. As you work with them you must consider three things:

1. The current position of the imaginary pointer.
2. Where you wish to move the pointer.
3. Whether you wish to trace a line as the pointer moves.

ILLUSTRATION 11.1

The DRAW Statement commands

Command	Meaning
Un	Move UP n PELs
Dn	Move DOWN n PELs
Ln	Move LEFT n PELs
Rn	Move RIGHT n PELs
En	Move diagonally UP and RIGHT n PELs
Fn	Move diagonally DOWN and RIGHT n PELs
Gn	Move diagonally DOWN and LEFT n PELs
Hn	Move diagonally UP and LEFT n PELs
M h,v	Move to location (h,v)
M $-h, -v$	Move left h PELs and up v PELs
M $+h, +v$	Move right h PELs and down v PELs
An	Rotate at angle n
Cn	Use color n from the current palette
Sn	Scale the figure up by n/4 when you draw it. Multiply the distances in the movement commands by n/4.
XV$	Execute the commands that have previously been stored in V$
Bc	Execute the movement command, c, but do not plot any points. B may be prefix to any of the movement commands.
Nc	Execute the movement command, c, and then return to the previous position. N may be a prefix for any of the movement commands.

The statement

```
10 DRAW "M160,100"
```

moves the imaginary pointer to the PEL at (160,100), tracing a path of lighted PELs as it does so.

```
10 DRAW "BM160,100"
```

moves the imaginary pointer to PEL at (160,100) without tracing its path. The B prefix makes moves invisible.

```
10 DRAW "M-10,+40"
```

moves the imaginary pointer from the last PEL referenced left ten positions and down 40 rows. M command values preceded by a plus or minus sign signify movement relative to the last PEL referenced. Otherwise, the M command values are the absolute coordinates of the destination of the move. Unless the M command is preceded by the B prefix, it lights PELs as it moves.

```
10 DRAW "L10,V10,R10,D10"
```

traces a line from the last PEL referenced left 10 PELs, up 10 PELs, right 10 PELs, and down 10 PELs, which creates a box outline.

The DRAW statement makes it possible to design components of shapes you will be using (such as legs, arms, hats) and then display them in various combinations over and over again in your program. You use special DRAW statement commands and store them in string variables that can be referenced whenever you need them.

Illustration 11.2 is a program that uses the DRAW statement to create a bug. Lines 40 through 110 define the creature's components: a body and leg, another leg, arms, neck, head, and feelers. Lines 200 through 370 move an imaginary pointer around the screen and execute the drawing instructions.

ILLUSTRATION 11.2

Using DRAW to create a creature

```
10  CLS
20  SCREEN 1,0
30  COLOR 9,0
35  REM DEFINE THE BUG
40  BDY$="BM=H;,=V;L20U20R20D20F10D10R2"
50  LEG$="BM=H;,=V;G10D10L2"
60  ARM1$="BM=H;,=V;L10D10L2"
70  ARM2$="BM=H;,=V;E10H10R2"
80  NECK$="BM=H;,=V;U4"
90  HEAD$="BM=H;,=V;R10H6G6"
100 FLR1$="BM=H;,=V;H6"
110 FLR2$="BM=H;,=V;E6"
120 DRAW "C2"
200 REM DRAW THE BUG
210 H = 270
215 V = 150
220 DRAW "XBDY$;"
230 H = H-20
240 DRAW "XLEG$;"
250 V = V-20
260 DRAW "XARM1$;"
```

```
270 H = H+20
280 DRAW "XARM2$;"
290 H = H-10
300 DRAW "XNECK$;"
310 H = H-5
320 V = V-4
330 DRAW "XHEAD$;"
340 V = V-3
350 DRAW "XFLR1$;"
360 H = H+7
370 DRAW "XFLR2$;"
380 END
```

Illustration 11.2 also shows the steps to follow when using the DRAW statement:

1. Define the string

   ```
   80 NECK$ = "BM=H;,=V;U4"
   ```

   Note that variables like H and V can be used as M command values. When they are, they must be preceded by an equal sign (=) and followed by a semicolon (;).

2. Set the color

   ```
   120 DRAW "C2"
   ```

   This sets the color for the following DRAW statements. Here, the second color of the chosen palette will be used.

3. Set the location

   ```
   230 H = H-20
   ```

   H is a variable representing the horizontal location of the starting PEL for the next shape to be drawn. This statement reduces the value of H so the leg drawn by the next statement appears in the correct place twenty PELs to the left.

4. Execute the command

   ```
   220 DRAW "XBDY$"
   ```

   The X command executes the commands previously stored in BDY$. They are the ones that draw the body of the bug.

Notice that the DRAW statement parameters are always surrounded by quotation marks. They are actually strings which are composed of commands, constants, or string variables.

Using variables in the DRAW statement saves a lot of work. Illustration 11.3 puts four bugs on the screen with about as many lines of program code as were used in the previous illustration for only one creature. The horizontal and vertical locations change as the FOR . . . NEXT loop proceeds so that for each iteration of the loop, the DRAW statements are executed in a different spot and a new bug appears.

ILLUSTRATION 11.3

Making use of variables in the DRAW statement move command

```
10 CLS
20 SCREEN 1,0
30 COLOR 9,0
35 REM DEFINE THE BUG
40 BDY$="BM=H;,=V;L20U20R20D20F10D10R2"
50 LEG$="BM=H;,=V;G10D10L2"
60 ARM1$="BM=H;,=V;L10D10L2"
70 ARM2$="BM=H;,=V;E10H10R2"
80 NECK$="BM=H;,=V;U4"
90 HEAD$="BM=H;,=V;R10H6G6"
100 FLR1$="BM=H;,=V;H6"
110 FLR2$="BM=H;,=V;E6"
120 DRAW "C2"
130 REM SET STARTING POINT
140 H = 319                        ←— new
150 V = 199                        ←— new
160 REM DRAW FOUR TIMES
170 FOR X = 1 TO 4                 ←— new
180 H = H-50
190 V = V-20
200 REM DRAW THE BUG
220 DRAW "XBDY$;"
230 H = H-20
240 DRAW "XLEG$;"
250 V = V-20
260 DRAW "XARM1$;"
270 H = H +20
280 DRAW "XARM2$;"
290 H = H-10
300 DRAW "XNECK$;"
310 H = H-5
320 V = V-4
330 DRAW "XHEAD$;"
```

```
340 V = V-3
350 DRAW "XFLR1$;"
360 H = H+7
370 DRAW "XFLR2$;"
380 NEXT X                    ←── new
390 END
```

Animated Displays

The GET and PUT statements provide an easy way to animate a
screen display. They work by letting you lift a section of the screen
from one location and place it in another. The change is rapid
because the original shape is copied PEL for PEL and not redrawn
by re-executing the original sequence of LINE, CIRCLE, PAINT,
or DRAW statements.

Illustration 11.4 lets the bug hop around the screen by first using
GET to store the bug design and then using PUT to copy it wherever
you wish to see it on the screen. The sense of movement is created
because the bug is erased between each hop.

ILLUSTRATION 11.4

Using GET and PUT to create animation

```
10 CLS
20 SCREEN 1,0
30 COLOR 9,0
35 REM DEFINE THE BUG
40 BDY$="BM=H;,=V;L20U20R20D20F10D10R2"
50 LEG$="BM=H;,=V;G10D10L2"
60 ARM1$="BM=H;,=V;L10D10L2"
70 ARM2$="BM=H;,=V;E10H10R2"
80 NECK$="BM=H;,=V;U4"
90 HEAD$="BM=H;,=V;R10H6G6"
100 FLR1$="BM=H;,=V;H6"
110 FLR2$="BM=H;,=V;E6"
120 DRAW "C2"
200 REM DRAW THE BUG
210 H = 160
215 V = 100
220 DRAW "XBDY$;"
230 H = H-20
240 DRAW "XLEG$;"
250 V = V-20
260 DRAW "XARM1$;"
```

```
270 H = H+20
280 DRAW "XARM2$;"
290 H = H-10
300 DRAW "XNECK$;"
310 H = H-5
320 V = V-4
330 DRAW "XHEAD$;"
340 V = V-3
350 DRAW "XFLR1$;"
360 H = H+7
370 DRAW "XFLR2$;"
375 PAINT (158,98),2,2
380 BYTES =INT((55*2+7)/8)*60
385 DIM BUG(BYTES)
390 GET (119,120)-(174,60),BUG
395 CLS
400 PUT (250,80),BUG
405 PUT (250,80),BUG
410 PUT (30,60),BUG
415 PUT (30,60),BUG
420 PUT (160,130),BUG
425 PUT (160,130),BUG
430 PUT (180,70),BUG
440 PUT (180,70),BUG
450 END
```

The GET Statement

Before the GET statement executes, some important ground work must be done. You must determine dimensions of the area you wish to move and where it is located on the screen. Drawing a preliminary design on graph paper, where each square represents a PEL on the screen, helps a great deal.

The GET statement works by copying an area of the screen into an array. Thus, the array must be DIMensioned before the GET statement executes. There is a formula for determining how big an array to use which takes into account the size of the area and whether you are using the medium- or high-resolution screen.

```
INT((horizontal PELs * 2 + 7)/8) * vertical PELs
```

is the formula for the medium-resolution screen.

```
INT((horizontal PELs + 7)/8) * vertical PELs
```

is the formula for the high-resolution screen.

Line 380 of Illustration 11.4 calculates the array size for the bug design using the formula for medium resolution. It is approximately 55 PELs wide and 60 PELs high. The result of this calculation becomes the dimension value for the array, BUG in line 385.

```
390 GET (119,120) - (174,60), BUG
```

copies the rectangular area with the lower leftmost PEL (119,120) and the upper rightmost PEL (174,60) into the elements of the array, BUG.

The PUT Statement

Now, it becomes a simple matter to very quickly PUT copies of the bug wherever you wish to see them. Lines 400 to 430 place the array contents at the locations denoted by the coordinates in the PUT statements.

```
415 PUT (250,80), BUG
```

copies the area retrieved by the GET onto the area of the screen that has PEL (250,80) as its upper leftmost corner. Two identical PUT statements in a row write and then erase an image. Thus, the second PUT (250,80), BUG statement in line 405 erases the bug and leaves the background unchanged. The series of double PUTs that write and erase in rapid succession make the bug appear to move.

Put statement parameters

The PUT statement has parameters that determine how the image you are creating will react with the existing background.

```
10 PUT (250,80), BUG, PSET
```

writes the image onto the background.

```
10 PUT (250,80), BUG, PRESET
```

writes the negative of the original image onto the background.

```
10 PUT (250,80), BUG,XOR
```

acts as PUT with no final parameter. Two such statements in a row write and then erase the image without changing the background.

```
10 PUT (250,80), BUG, AND
```

writes the image only if another already exists in the new location.

The new image replaces the previous image.

```
10 PUT (250,80), BUG, OR
```

superimposes the new image onto an existing image. Take some time to experiment with these fancy PUT statement features.

The POINT Function

You can find out the color number of any PEL by giving its coordinates as the argument of the POINT (,) function.

```
10 PRINT POINT (155,99)
```

produces a 0, 1, 2, or 3 in medium-resolution graphics to indicate either the background (0) or one of the current palette colors. In high resolution, POINT returns 0 for the background and 1 for white.

The BEEP Statement

```
10 BEEP
```

Perhaps the most simple of the BASIC statements, but a very effective one, BEEP emits sound from the terminal's speaker for a quarter of a second. It has the same effect as PRINT CHR$(7). Executing several BEEPs in succession creates a sustained noise which will draw someone's attention if your program requires it. Experiment with:

```
10 FOR X = 1 TO 10
20     BEEP
30 NEXT X
```

The SOUND Statement

ILLUSTRATION 11.5

SOUND effects

```
10 FOR X = 37 TO 3000 STEP 100
20     SOUND X, 18
30 NEXT X
40 END
```

RUN the program in Illustration 11.5 to hear how the SOUND statement works. It produces sound at the frequency and for the duration you specify. The first parameter, X, sets the frequency. It can be in the range of 37 to 32767, although you may not enjoy or even be able to hear the upper ranges.

The second parameter, 18, sets the duration by specifying a number of computer clock ticks. Because there are 18.2 ticks in a second, this example emits the sound at each frequency for about one second.

Normally a SOUND statement waits for the preceding SOUND statement to finish before making the sound it is written to produce. However, a SOUND statement with a duration of zero does not produce any sound of its own, but rather interrupts any preceding SOUND statement by turning its sound off even if it has not RUN for the duration specified.

The PLAY Statement

The PLAY statement makes it possible to compose musical phrases and play them in various combinations as your program runs. As with the DRAW statement, PLAY has its own set of tune definition commands. They allow you to set the tempo, the octave, the pauses and many other musical attributes of a tune. Combine these commands into string constants and assign them to a string variable. When you wish them to be heard, refer to the variable in a PLAY statement X command.

Illustration 11.6 is a program that uses the PLAY statement to re-create a familiar tune. Lines 10 through 40 defines its phrases; lines 50 and 60 execute them.

ILLUSTRATION 11.6

PLAYing "Happy Birthday"

```
10 FIRST$ = "L8 MF MS 03 GG L4 AG 04 C 03 L2 B"
20 SECOND$ = "L8 MF MS 03 GG L4 AG 04 D L2 C"
30 THIRD$ = "L8 MF MS 03 GG L4 04 GE L8 CC 03 L4 B A"
40 FOURTH$ = "04 L8 FF L4 ECD L1 C"
50 PLAY "XFIRST$; XSECOND$;"
60 PLAY "XTHIRD$; XFOURTH$;"
```

All of the PLAY statement commands appear in Illustration 11.7. As you use them you will see that they allow you a great deal of flexibility in creating musical compositions. Reflect a minute on the ingenuity of the computer scientists who have found yet another way to use the binary code!

ILLUSTRATION 11.7

The PLAY statement commands

Command	Meaning
A to G	Play the note indicated by the letter.
A to G followed by #, +, or −	Play the note indicated by the letter and the sign: # or + (means sharp) − (means flat)
Ln	Play the notes that follow for an interval of 1/n each. n is in the range of 1 to 64. L1 is a whole note.
On	Set the octave to octave n. Octave 3 starts with middle C. There are seven octaves (0 to 6); each one goes from C to B.
Pn	Rest, or pause, for an interval of 1/n where n may range from 1 to 64.
Tn	Set the tempo, or number of quarter notes in a second. n may range from 32 to 255. The default is 120.
Nn	Play note n which may range from 0 to 84. Each of the octaves has 12 notes including sharps and flats. 0 signifies rest.
MN	Music Normal. Each note plays 7/8 of the time specified by L.
ML	Music Legato. Each note plays the full interval specified by L.
MS	Music Staccato. Each note plays 3/4 of the time specified by L.
MF	Music Foreground. Each note created by PLAY or SOUND will wait until the previous note is finished. Program execution halts until playing has finished. This is the default.
MB	Music Background. Each note created by PLAY or SOUND is stored in a buffer and emitted while the rest of the program runs.

Background music is an extremely effective way of adding to computer results or calming an impatient customer who must wait (while the dating program, for example, progresses). Illustration 11.8 uses background music to personalize the birthday greeting of Illustration 11.6. In the phrase definition, lines 20 through 50, the command MF for foreground has been replaced by MB. As a result, the program does not wait for the music to complete before displaying the identity of the birthday fellow. Rather, the music is released while the FOR . . . NEXT loop proceeds. Jimmy's name is displayed while his music is playing in the background.

ILLUSTRATION 11.8

PLAYing background music

```
10 CLS
20 FIRST$ = "L8 MB MS O3 GG L4 AG O4 C O3 L2 B"
30 SECOND$ = "L8 MB MS O3 GG L4 AG O4 D L2 C"
40 THIRD$ = "L8 MB MS O3 GG L4 O4 GE L8 CC O3 L4 B A"
50 FOURTH$ = "O4 L8 FF L4 ECD L1 C"
60 PLAY "XFIRST$; XSECOND$; XTHIRD$; X FOURTH$;"
70 FOR X = 1 TO 24
80    PRINT "JAMES ARTHUR"
90 NEXT X
100 END
```

Finally, Illustration 11.9 shows that you do not need to use the X command to activate the PLAY commands. Include them directly in the PLAY statement if you wish. Line 20 also illustrates that arguments in PLAY statement commands can be variables as well as constants. The only requirement is that they be preceded by an equal (=) sign and followed by a semicolon (;).

ILLUSTRATION 11.9

Using variables in PLAY commands

```
10 FOR X = 1 TO 64
20    PLAY "L=X;O3G"
30 NEXT X
40 END
```

Here, X, the control variable of the FOR . . . NEXT loop, is used within the loop as the length of G note played in octave 3.

Notice that it is preceded by an equal sign and followed by a semicolon. Because the argument of the length (L) command sets the denominator of the fraction that represents the time interval of each note, this program, with larger and larger values of X, produces shorter and shorter notes. RUN it and see whether it reminds you of a bouncing ball.

Unusual Input

The INKEY$ function

Usually computer users enter data at the keyboard in response to an INPUT statement. This means that they must press at least two keys: one for the character they wish to send and another, the ENTER key, which actually transmits their data. In this process, a ? prompt and the character they typed are echoed on the screen.

The INKEY$ function eliminates the ? prompt, the echo, and the need to press ENTER. Illustration 11.10 shows a segment of a program that uses this function to allow a user to press number keys to show the direction they wish to travel:

2 means GO SOUTH
8 means GO NORTH
4 means GO WEST
6 means GO EAST

(These numbers correspond to the positions of the arrow keys on the numeric keyboard on the right side of the IBM personal computer keyboard.)

ILLUSTRATION 11.10

Sample program segment using INKEY$

```
10 PRINT "WHICH DIRECTION"
20 D$ = INKEY$
25 IF D$ = "" THEN 20
30 ON VAL(D$) GO TO 100,40,100,50,100,60,100,70,100
40 PRINT "YOU ARE NOW HEADING SOUTH"
45 GO TO ...southern routine
50 PRINT "YOU ARE NOW HEADING WEST"
55 GO TO ...western routine
60 PRINT "YOU ARE NOW HEADING EAST"
65 GO TO ...eastern routine
```

```
70 PRINT "YOU ARE NOW HEADING NORTH"
75 GO TO ...northern routine
100 PRINT "WRONG KEY"
   .
   .
   .

RUN

WHICH DIRECTION
YOU ARE NOW HEADING EAST
```

In lines 20 and 25 the program loops back to the statement with INKEY$ until something is entered at the keyboard. Unlike INPUT, INKEY$ does not cause program execution to halt. Rather, once a key is pressed the character it represents is stored as a string character in D$. Then, because this program expects numeric input, the VAL( ) function converts the character to its number equivalent on the ON . . . GO TO statement, and branching occurs. The RUN shows that the screen displays no evidence of the input transaction.

Light pens

The light pen is an input device that works by setting PELs when it touches the display screen. The statements that allow your program to detect its position are the PEN and ON . . . PEN statements and the PEN ( ) function.

The PEN statement

The PEN statement enables and disables the ON PEN GO SUB statement and *must* execute before an ON PEN GO SUB statement can process a light pen input.

Similarly, the statement

```
10 PEN OFF
```

should execute when the pen is no longer needed. It eliminates the need for the computer to check for pen input every time BASIC starts to evaluate a new statement.

```
10 PEN STOP
```

controls pen input by storing the most recent pen input until the ON PEN GO SUB routine has finished processing the current pen stroke. PEN STOP disables further trapping of pen activity.

The ON PEN GO SUB statement

Like ON ERROR GO TO, the ON PEN GO SUB statement interrupts processing when a pen stroke occurs and sends control to the subroutine, which takes appropriate action.

```
10 ON PEN GO SUB 100
       .
       .
       .
100 REM PEN SUBROUTINE
       .
       .
       .
150 RETURN
```

The subroutine at line 100 executes if a pen stroke occurs. If another pen event occurs while control is in the subroutine, an automatic PEN STOP occurs delaying processing of the new pen stroke until the current pen subroutine is finished.

```
10 ON PEN GO SUB 0
```

like PEN OFF, this statement (with a 0 line number) disables pen trapping. Further pen strokes will be ignored.

The PEN( ) function

The PEN( ) function gives you information about the position of the pen stroke.

```
10 X = PEN( )
```

gives X a numeric value according to the chart in Illustration 11.11.

Joysticks

Two joysticks (each having a steering mechanism and an associated trigger) are other input devices that BASIC can recognize. The statements STRIG, STRIG( ), and ON STRIG( ) GO SUB and the functions STRIG( ) and STICK( ) inform your program about joystick input. In the discussion of all of these statements the value ( ) can be either 0 for the joystick A or 2 for joystick B.

The STRIG( ) statement

This statement controls whether the ON STRIG( ) GO SUB statement is active.

```
10 STRIG( ) ON
```

ILLUSTRATION 11.11

PEN( ) function values

PEN( ) function	Value returned
X = PEN(0)	−1 = pen has been down since the last PEN(0) check. 0 = pen has been up since the last PEN(0) check.
X = PEN(1)	X contains the horizontal PEL address of the last pen event. For medium resolution this is in the range of 0 to 319. For high resolution it is in the range of 0 to 639.
X = PEN(2)	X contains the vertical coordinate of the last pen event. The range is from 0 to 199 for either medium or high resolution.
X = PEN(3)	−1 = the pen switch is down. 0 = the pen switch is up.
X = PEN(4)	X contains the last known valid horizontal pen coordinate.
X = PEN(5)	X contains the last known valid vertical pen coordinate.
X = PEN(6)	X = the text screen row where the pen was last activated. It can be in the range of 1 to 24.
X = PEN(7)	X = the text character position where the pen was last activated. It can range from 0 to 80.
X = PEN(8)	X = the last known valid text row.
X = PEN(9)	X = the last known valid text character position.

where (n) is 0 for joystick A or 2 for joystick B, allows the ON STRIG( ) GO SUB statement to check whether the trigger for A or B has been fired.

```
10 STRIG(n) OFF
```

disables the ON STRIG( ) GO SUB statement for the joystick specified in ( ).

```
10 STRIG(n) STOP
```

controls the stream of input for a particular joystick. It stores the fact that the trigger has been pushed, but does not make it available to the ON STRIG( ) GO SUB statement until that statement finishes processing the current trigger shot.

The ON STRIG( ) GO SUB statement

```
10 ON STRIG(2) GO SUB 100
```

Like ON PEN GO SUB, ON STRIG( ) GO SUB interrupts your program and sends control to the appropriate subroutine depending on whether the trigger for joystick A or B has been pressed. While control is in the routine, any other trigger press is delayed until the current shot has been completely processed. Upon return from the subroutine, any pending trigger press will be recognized and, if necessary, ON STRIG( ) executes another time.

The STRIG statement and the STRIG( ) function

```
10 STRIG ON
   .
   .
   .
40 X = STRIG( )
```

The statement STRIG ON must execute before the STRIG( ) function can work. When it is active, STRIG( ) returns a number between 0 and 1 that tells you about the status of the joystick A trigger (or between 2 and 3 for joystick B), according to the chart in Illustration 11.12. The statement STRIG OFF deactivates the STRIG( ) function.

ILLUSTRATION 11.12

STRIG( ) function values

STRIG( ) function	Values returned
X = STRIG(0)	X = 1 if button A was pressed since the last STRIG(0) statement. X = 0 if button A was not pressed since the last STRIG(0) statement.
X = STRIG(1)	X = 1 if button A is currently pressed. X = 0 if button A is not currently pressed.
X = STRIG(2)	X = 1 if button B was pressed since the last STRIG(2) statement. X = 0 if button B was not pressed since the last STRIG(2) statement.
X = STRIG(3)	X = 1 if button B is currently pressed. X = 0 if button B is not currently pressed.

The STICK( ) function

The STICK( ) function lets you keep track of the movement of the cursor controlled by either available joystick. Depending on the value of ( ), which you supply, it returns the X or Y coordinate of the cursor for joystick A or B. (The range of X and Y coordinates depends upon your computer.) Illustration 11.13 lists the possible STICK( ) function values.

ILLUSTRATION 11.13

STICK( ) function values

STICK( ) function	Values returned
C = STICK(0)	C = X coordinate for Joystick A
C = STICK(1)	C = Y coordinate for Joystick A
C = STICK(2)	C = X coordinate for Joystick B
C = STICK(3)	C = Y coordinate for Joystick B

Part Five

Data Files

Chapter 12

Disk File Concepts

Disks are the library of the computer system. During a computing session the memory (RAM) and the CPU are alive with data, calculations, and programs. With disks or other similar storage devices, these things can be permanently recorded. Without them, all that you have done is forgotten when you sign off.

The IBM personal computer BASIC statements needed to use disk files are very powerful; they give you complete control over your computer's storage facilities. This chapter lays a foundation of data file processing concepts for you. It introduces the data type definition statements: DEFINT, DEFSNG, DEFDBL and DEFSTR. Once you understand the computer processes that occur and the programmer's role in these processes, making data files work for you is as straightforward as cooking with a recipe.

Computer Processes

Illustration 12.1 shows the path that data travels through a computer system when it is being written on the disk.

1. Information you create at an input device (or a result produced by the CPU) is copied into the RAM.
2. As soon as your intention to store the information on the disk is known, your data is copied into a portion of RAM called the buffer. This serves as a terminus for data transfer to and from the disk.

183

3. Data traverses an input/output (I/O) channel from the buffer to a designated disk file. There may be channels between various files and various buffers open at one time.
4. Data is coded onto the disk surface as tiny spots magnetized in a clockwise or counterclockwise direction. (Once valuable information is stored on the disk, protect its surface and keep it away from the magnetic field created by electric motors and magnets.)

ILLUSTRATION 12.1

Writing (output) to a data file in a disk-based computer system

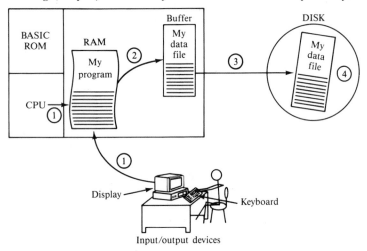

Illustration 12.2 shows that when disk files are read, data follows the reverse path:

1. Data traverses the input/output (I/O) channel from the disk to the file buffer in RAM.
2. Data flows from the buffer in the RAM where it is processed by your program.
3. Data is sent from the RAM to the display screen or printer.

Keep these flows in your mind's eye as you work with the disk.

Programming Processes

Manipulating data files requires a computer program to accomplish five important tasks:

1. *Associate a file name with a channel and declare it OPEN.* BASIC has an OPEN statement which takes care of this. In its simplest form, OPEN includes only the name of the disk file you intend to use. It may require other information about the file.

2. *Declare the file open for input or output.* The computer needs to know whether you will be writing into the file, reading existing file data, or possibly doing both. When you are asked to specify this, keep in mind the following directions for disk file I/O:

    INPUT = from the disk to the program in RAM.
    OUTPUT = from the program to the disk file.

3. *Declare the file for sequential or random (direct) access.* It makes a big difference to the computer whether you plan to retrieve your file data in sequence or whether you will retrieve an item directly without reading preceding items.

4. *Transfer data.* Usually variations of the PRINT and INPUT statements take care of this. BASIC has GET and PUT statements for disk data transfer as well.

5. *CLOSE the channel to the file.* There is a CLOSE statement for this.

ILLUSTRATION 12.2

Reading (input) from a data file in a disk-based computer system

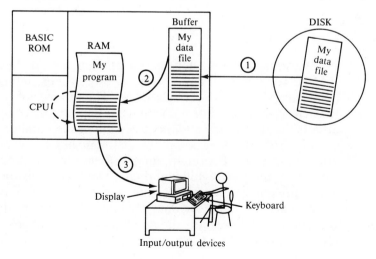

Physical Records, File Records, and Fields

The programmer's vocabulary includes two types of records: physical records and file records.

A *physical record* is the smallest number of bytes that is transferred to or from the disk in one data transfer operation. On the IBM personal computer a physical record has 512 bytes. The file buffer holds one physical record. Every write-to-disk operation writes out one record; every read operation copies one physical record into the buffer.

A *file record* is a conceptual unit of file information, and its size depends upon the programming project at hand. It is the entire package of information about an item in the file. A file record is composed of *fields,* or units of data, pertaining to the item. In a dentist's file where the items are patients, one file record contains all of the information for one patient. This record might be composed of several fields: a name field, an age field, a phone number field, and a number-of-cavities-filled field.

Physical records and file records rarely match. File records may be greater or smaller than one physical record. Usually, they are smaller. Data processing is very efficient when several file records fit exactly into one physical record.

You will frequently come across the term *record* as you read the literature for your computer. Be sure to determine whether the reference is to physical or file records. IBM personal computer documents usually call *physical records,* Sectors; *file records,* Records; and *fields,* Data items.

Data Types

For various reasons such as the efficient use of memory space, BASIC considers all data as one of three types: integers, floating-point numbers, or ASCII characters. The number of bytes allocated to each type varies. For numeric data, the number of bytes allocated affects the magnitude and the precision of the number represented.

The IBM personal computer distinguishes between single- and double-precision floating-point numbers. Single-precision uses 4 bytes and allows 6 significant digits. Double-precision uses 8 bytes and represents at least 16 significant digits. The symbol attached to the variable name or data constant determines the data type. Illustration 12.3 presents the number of bytes, ranges, and symbols for the various data types on the IBM personal computer.

ILLUSTRATION 12.3

IBM personal computer data types

Integers	
Number of Bytes	2
Range	−32768 − +32767
Sample variable	N%
Sample constant	8%
Single-precision floating point	
Number of bytes	4
Range	±2.9E38 − ±1.7E38
Significant digits	6
Sample variable	N or N!
Sample constant	5.6 or 5.6!
Double-precision floating point	
Number of bytes	8
Range	±2.9E38 − ±1.7E38
Significant digits	16
Sample variable	N#
Sample constant	14#
Characters	
Number of bytes	1
Sample variable	N$
Sample constant	"H"
Hexidecimal numbers	
Number of bytes	2
Range	−32768 − +65535
Sample variable	N
Sample constant	&H76
Octal numbers	
Number of bytes	2
Range	−32768 − +65535
Sample variable	N
Sample constant	&123

The DEFtype Statements

The DEFINT, DEFSNG, DEFDBL, and DEFSTR statements declare whole groups of variables as integers, single-precision, double-precision or strings respectively. Thus,

```
10 DEFINT C, V-Z
```

establishes all variables beginning with C, V, W, X, Y, and Z as integer variables. The DEFtype statements must come at the beginning of your program. When you use DEFtype statements you no longer need to append the data type symbols (#, !, %, or $) to the variable names.

File Design: The File Record Layout

Before beginning to use any type of file, you must think about— and write down—the length and type of data that will comprise the file records. The document you create, often called the File Record layout, will be referenced time and again during the life of the file. Because it maps the bytes in one file record, you can use it to calculate in advance how many physical records on the disk the file will require. It specifies the type of data involved, so you know what variables you can use. What is more important, a file record layout allows you or other programmers, at a future time, to use the file in another program. If you cannot remember how a file is organized, you cannot retrieve its data.

Illustration 12.4 shows a file record layout designed for an IBM personal computer file of 24 swimmers. It describes the layout of one file record and summarizes the file dimensions. Each file record contains a name, team, and swim event field as well as an age field and a field to store the swimmer's best swimming time.

ILLUSTRATION 12.4

File record layout

File name: SWIMER	File type: SEQUENTIAL		Contents: 24 swimmers
Variable name	Description of field	Field length bytes	Data type
N$	Swimmer's name	30	30 characters
T$	Swimmer's team	20	20 characters
E$	Swimmer's event	8	8 characters
A$	Swimmer's age	2	Integer
T	Swimmer's best time	4	Single-precision decimal
		Total: 64	

Summary: 64 bytes per file record
8 file records per physical record
24 swimmers = 3 physical records (sectors)

The length and data type of each field are also listed along with the variables in the computer programs which use these file records. There is no programming need to use the same variable in all of the programs that access the file. But having such consistency makes it easy to keep track of what these programs do with the file information.

Notice the summary in the file layout. It shows that 24 64-byte file records use 3 physical records on the IBM personal computer.

Sequential and Random Access

Computers are capable of either sequential or random access file processing. With sequential files, data must be read in the same order as they were written into the file. If you want to read the ninth file record, you must pull out and pass by the first eight file records. Random (direct) access files allow you to skip around, reading and updating file records without regard to their positions in the file.

If you plan to use almost all of your file data each time the file is opened, and you will not frequently change its contents, choose sequential files. These are probably the easiest to program and are certainly the most efficient for the computer. You need random access files if you will frequently update the file records and want to look at them out of sequence. Store mailing lists, where every name in the file is printed on a label, in sequential files. Store theater reservations that change for each performance in random access files.

Problems

Complete each sentence with a short phrase.

1. The buffer is located in _____.

2. Magnetic disks and tapes are useful for long-term storage

   of computer information because _____

   _____.

3. The five tasks necessary when writing to data files are:

_____

_____

_____

_____

_____.

4. A physical record is _____.

5. A file record is _____.

6. A file record layout describes _____

_____.

7. Sequential access files are so named because they _____

_____.

8. Random access files are so named because they _____

_____.

9. Give an example of a computer use that is best suited to sequential access files and an example of a use best suited to random access files.

_____

_____

_____

10. Make a chart listing the data types your computer uses. Show the number of bytes it allows for each and give an example of a variable and a constant for each data type.

Chapter 13

Sequential Files

The computer views sequential files as collections of data fields separated by a marker, such as a comma or the ENTER code. You, as the programmer, must give the structure to these data fields.

When you write into the file, use the file record layout to remind yourself of the sequence of data fields that should comprise each file record. Write out the fields for one file record and then begin again for another record until all of the information is in the file.

Read the file with a programming routine that parallels the writing routine. In fact, it is a good idea to match them exactly. If the write routine includes a line like:

```
10 PRINT#1, "DAFFODILS",4.50, "PER DOZEN"
```

the read routine should look like:

```
20 INPUT#1, A$, B, D$
```

That is, the number of fields and their data type for the PRINT are matched by the number of fields and their type in the corresponding INPUT statement (a character string, a number, a character string). It is also a good idea to work with one complete file record in each read operation. You may use only part of the information you have accessed, but you will have an easy time keeping track of your place in the file.

Illustration 13.1 sets up a sports file. It prompts for game names and writes them into a disk file called GAMES.

ILLUSTRATION 13.1

Entering data in a sequential file

```
10 OPEN "GAMES" FOR OUTPUT AS #1
20 FOR X = 1 TO 5
30 INPUT "ENTER A GAME NAME";F$
40 PRINT #1, F$
50 NEXT X
60 CLOSE #1
70 END

RUN

ENTER A GAME NAME? SOCCER
ENTER A GAME NAME? GOLF
ENTER A GAME NAME? FOOTBALL
ENTER A GAME NAME? BASKETBALL
ENTER A GAME NAME? RUGBY
```

Line 10 sets up a channel FOR OUTPUT. That is, for data transfer from the buffer to the file GAMES. Use FOR OUTPUT *only once* in the life of the file. This tells the computer you are writing a new file. If the file you name already exists, the computer will erase its contents and set you up for a "fresh start." Later sections of this chapter explain how to add new information to an existing sequential file.

The channel designator (the #1 in the OPEN statement in Illustration 13.1) serves to distinguish this channel from others that might be open at the same time by this program. Ordinarily, you have a maximum of 3 files which may be open at once, but you can increase this to up to 15 channels when you request the BASIC language at start-up time. In response to the DOS command prompt, enter:

```
BASIC/F:15
```

or, for Advanced BASIC

```
BASICA/F:15
```

Every channel you allocate requires some main storage for control information, so you should not request more file channels than you think you'll need.

In your program, channel numbers may be in the range of 1 to 15. It makes no difference which number you choose for a file;

the important thing is that you use the same one each time you refer to your file during the RUN of a program. In another program, you can use a different channel designator for the same file.

The PRINT # statement in line 40 tells the computer to write the current value of F$ to the buffer for the file associated with channel 1. All PRINT statements not followed by a comma or a semicolon generate the carriage return character CHR$(13). Because this printing is ultimately directed to the disk, CHR$(13) is written in the buffer as well. It becomes the separator that the computer uses to distinguish this file record from the next one in the file.

While this file is open, the contents of the buffer is copied to the disk each time all of its 512 bytes are filled. Line 60, the CLOSE statement, writes out even a partially filled buffer and closes access to the file.

Reading from a Sequential File

Illustration 13.2 reads from the sports file. It displays the games that have been stored within.

ILLUSTRATION 13.2

Reading a sequential file

```
10 OPEN "GAMES" FOR INPUT AS #2
20 FOR X = 1 TO 5
30    INPUT #2, G$
40    PRINT G$
50 NEXT X
60 CLOSE #2
70 END

RUN

SOCCER
GOLF
FOOTBALL
BASKETBALL
RUGBY
```

The FOR INPUT specification in the OPEN statement in line 10 of Illustration 13.2 makes this the counterpart of the OPEN statement that wrote into the file. This says, prepare to read the file by transferring data from the file on the disk to the buffer in RAM. INPUT # also refers to data transfer over the channel from the disk to the buffer. Line 30 in this illustration reads one complete record from the file GAMES associated with channel 2 into the variable G$. Line 40 displays it on the screen.

File Records and Their Fields

Think of BASIC as viewing all of the information in one PRINT # statement as comprising one file record. Each field within the record is represented by a single variable and separated from the next field by a comma. For example, a file record composed of three fields—S$ for a dress style, C$ for a dress color, and P for its price—would be written out as:

```
10 PRINT #1, S$;",";C$;",";P
```

The PRINT # statement in the write program must be matched by an INPUT # in the read program that transmits the same amount and type of data. Here, PRINT # writes out two character strings and a decimal number. In the retrieval program, the INPUT # must read in two character strings and a decimal number:

```
10 INPUT #1, S$,C$,P
```

The two programs in Illustration 13.3 write to and then read from the DRESS file. Each file record consists of these three fields.

ILLUSTRATION 13.3

Accessing sequential file records composed of three fields

```
10 OPEN "DRESS" FOR OUTPUT AS #1
20 FOR X = 1 TO 5
30 INPUT "ENTER A DRESS";S$,C$,P
40 PRINT #1,S$;",";C$;",";P
50 NEXT X
60 CLOSE #1
70 END

RUN

ENTER A DRESS? A35,RED,68.95
ENTER A DRESS? A36,BLUE,75
ENTER A DRESS? B44,PINK,105.50
```

```
ENTER A DRESS? C78,GRAY,85
ENTER A DRESS? BL5,BLACK,78.89

10 OPEN "DRESS" FOR INPUT AS #2
20 FOR X = 1 TO 5
30    INPUT #2, S$,C$,P
40    PRINT S$,C$,P
50 NEXT X
60 CLOSE #2
70 END

RUN

A35    RED      68.95
A36    BLUE     75
B44    PINK     105.5
C78    GRAY     85
BL5    BLACK    78.89
```

The WRITE # Statement

The WRITE # statement makes it easy to enter file records composed of several fields. You do not have to carefully write the commas that will separate fields in the file in your PRINT # statement. The WRITE # statement does this work for you. Use it instead of PRINT #. Replace line 40 of Illustration 13.3 with:

```
40 WRITE #1, S$, C$, P
```

You need only concern yourself with using the proper variables to represent the file data.

Updating a Sequential File

Changing an item, deleting something, or extending an existing sequential file requires opening two files: the one to be updated and a new one which will become the revised version of the old file. Ultimately, the original file will be deleted. In Illustration 13.4, the program changes BASKETBALL in the GAMES file to WATER POLO.

ILLUSTRATION 13.4

Updating a sequential file

```
10 OPEN "GAMES" FOR INPUT AS #1
20 OPEN "GAMES2" FOR OUTPUT AS #2
30 FOR X = 1 TO 5
40     INPUT #1, F$
50     IF F$ = "BASKETBALL" THEN F$ = "WATER POLO"
60     PRINT #2, F$
70 NEXT X
80 CLOSE 1,2
90 KILL "GAMES"
100 NAME "GAMES2" AS "GAMES"
110 END
```

The original file, GAMES, and a new empty file, GAMES2, are opened in lines 10 and 20. Each item in GAMES is read and written to the new file if it is not BASKETBALL. When BASKETBALL is encountered, line 30 replaces it by assigning WATER POLO to F$. In line 60, this sport is the one written into the output file in place of BASKETBALL. After all of the original file has been read, the files are closed.

The final steps, erasing the original file and giving its name to the new file, ensure that any other programs expecting to find a file called GAMES will do so. Lines 90 and 100 erase the old file and change the new file's name.

Appending Data to a Sequential File

The FOR APPEND specification in the OPEN statement prepares the computer for output to the disk and sets the file pointer to the end of the file. Subsequent file writing statements extend the file to include the new information. Illustration 13.5 adds two sports to the GAMES file.

ILLUSTRATION 13.5

Appending data to a sequential file

```
LIST
10 OPEN "GAMES" FOR APPEND AS #1
20 PRINT #1, "LACROSSE"
30 PRINT #1, "TENNIS"
40 CLOSE #1
50 END
```

Problems

Programming problems

1. The Alumni Office uses a sequential file.
   a. Create a sequential file that will be useful for the Director of Alumni Affairs. Store the name, graduating class, favorite sport, and current occupation of each alumnus. (Use a sample of 10 alumni.)
   b. Use the file to print a letter of invitation to the State Swimming Championships to all of the alumni who are recorded as having named swimming as their favorite sport.

2. The Computer Company keeps a sequential file of its 20 employees.
   a. Create a sequential file that contains their names, street addresses, cities, states, and zip codes.
   b. Use the computer to print mailing labels for their weekly paychecks.

3. The Weather Bureau keeps the snowfall statistics for each county in a separate sequential file. Each file contains three pieces of information: the meteorologist's name, the county name, and the number of inches of snow for the season.
   a. First write the program, and then enter this data for three counties.
   b. Draw upon all three files to get the data to calculate the average snowfall for the three counties. Print the average on the screen.

4. The Internal Revenue Service has surprise refunds for all taxpayers who paid their income tax before the April deadline.
   a. Create a file with the names, payment dates, and amount of tax paid for each citizen. (Use a sample of six citizens.)
   b. Have the computer read the file and calculate a 10% refund for all pre-April payers. Print their names and the amounts of their refunds on the screen.

5. All of the retail stores who are customers of the Junk Jewelry Manufacturing Company are listed in the company's customer master file. It contains their names, cities, and designations of their credit standings. (P = poor, G = good.)
   a. Write the program that creates this sequential customer master file.
   b. Write a program that creates two new sequential files, GOOD and POOR, each containing the list of customers with good or poor ratings.
   c. Ask the bookkeeper whether he or she wishes to see the list of good customers or poor customers; print out the names and cities of everyone in the appropriate file.

6. Kenneth Bedford, prominent Metropolitan City attorney, uses the computer to keep track of his clients and their legal problems.
   a. Write the program that allows him to enter the following names, charges, and court decisions into a sequential file.

Name	Charge	Decision
Prof. Prune	Libel	Won!
Miss Rouge	Slander	Lost
Tom Tough	Arson	????
General Spice	Theft	Won!
Mrs. Knight	Bribery	Lost

   b. Tom Tough has gone from the frying pan into the fire. Write the program that updates this sequential file and change the decision for him from ???? to LOST.
   c. Print out the updated file.

7. The Mighty Metropolitan baseball team and the Sluggin' Scouts use the computer to store the names, at bats, and hits of each of the nine players on their teams in the team sequential files.
   a. Create the METRO file and the SCOUT file with this information.
   b. Draw from the data in these files to create another file, ALLSTAR, which contains the names, teams, and batting averages of the players from either team with the best batting average. ALLSTAR includes only the nine best batters. Print their names and batting averages on the screen as well.

8. By some well-kept secret, the names on the mailing lists from catalog sales companies always become part of the Master Junk Mail mailing list.
   a. Create a larger (10-name) MASTER sequential file and a smaller (5-name) FAMILY sequential file to represent the names for the junk mail list and the Family Mail Order Catalog file. Then append the Family mailing list to the Master list.
   b. Write the program that randomly picks one name from this sequential MASTER file and sends a letter telling the person that she has won the $10 million sweepstakes.

9. Use the computer to assign jobs to the campers at Camp Jolly Good Fun.
   a. Make sure that no one repeats a job until he has done all of the other jobs. Set up five sequential files, MON, TUES, WED, THURS, and FRI, to store the duty roster for each day of the week. Use a sample of five campers and five jobs for this exercise.
   b. Ask the camp director which day he wishes to see; print the duty roster that has been stored in the file for that day.

10. The school registrar uses the computer to store student academic records.
    a. Create and fill a sequential file with the name, course, and grade-point average of students in the courses at Highpoint High. Use the sample names below:

Name	Course	Average
Smith	French	98
Jones	English	45
Ocker	Math	56
Bell	French	87
Moral	English	98
Hawkins	English	91
Tremont	Math	99
Bosting	Math	78
Helms	Math	90
Goodie	English	78

    b. Select those students with averages above 89 to be stored in a special file: SMART.
    c. Allow the registrar to create advanced courses from the information in the file SMART. Have her enter the name of the course she is interested in, and have the computer list the students in the SMART file who are enrolled in the course she has requested.

Chapter 14

Random Access Files

Random access requires that file records and the fields within them be of a predetermined and fixed length. The computer finds a particular file record by using the established bytes per record to calculate its position in the file. Thus, the advantage of direct access is based upon the constraint that, at the outset, you establish file dimensions and make all of your data conform to these parameters. Usually, the most serious consequence of this is that disk space is wasted, since fields with short data are padded with blanks.

Random access files require that you, the programmer, direct the flow of every character in your file throughout the computer system. This has the advantage that since you have complete control of your data, you can "fine-tune" your files as you wish them to be. Because you serve as the traffic director, random access programming is one case in which the time you took to review the components of a computer system really pays off. If your mind has a vision of how things are related, your task is easy.

Various Data Types in Random Access Files

All information goes into the buffer and out to random access files as character string data. You must convert numbers to strings before you put them into the file and reconvert them when they are retrieved. BASIC includes functions that make these conversions

200

easy. All you need to remember is how many bytes each type of number requires:

Integers	2 bytes
Single-precision decimals	4 bytes
Double-precision decimals	8 bytes

Designing a Data File

Remember the concept of a physical record: it is the smallest number of bytes transmitted during a data transfer operation. On the IBM personal computer, physical records are called sectors and contain 512 bytes. A file record for an item in a user's file usually contains fewer bytes than a sector. As you work with random access files, you will need to know how many file records fit within a sector. You will also need to know all about the fields within the file record: how long they are, and whether they contain numeric or character data.

Thus, one of your first tasks is to complete a file record layout. Illustration 14.1 repeats the layout for the file of swimmers in Chapter 12.

ILLUSTRATION 14.1

File record layout

File name: SWIMER	File type: Record I/O		Contents: 24 swimmers
Variable name	*Description of field*	*Field length (bytes)*	*Data type*
N$	Swimmer's name	30	30 characters
T$	Swimmer's team	20	20 characters
E$	Swimmer's event	8	8 characters
A$	Swimmer's age	2	1 integer
T$	Swimmer's best time	4	1 single-precision decimal
		Total: 64	

Summary: 64 bytes/logical record
8 logical records/physical records
24 swimmers = 3 physical records (sectors)

When you write the program that will access the data in this file, the layout will be extremely helpful. It shows, for example, that each file record uses 64 bytes; this is information that you want to include in the random access file OPEN statement.

The layout also shows that each sector holds 8 swimmers' file records. As you design your file, keep in mind the relationship between the size of the sector and the size of the file record. Ideally, they will be the same; access to any one file record is then most efficient. However, you do not want to make file records larger than they actually need to be. With some thought, you can plan the file records to be even multiples of 512, as shown in Illustration 14.1. This improves file processing performance.

If you do not specify otherwise, the computer gives you a default file record length of 128 bytes. You can change this by adding the record length specifier to the OPEN statement.

```
10 OPEN "EASY" AS #1 LEN = 512
```

gives you a file record of 512 bytes. Each time you open the file you will need to use the same length modifier.

If you need a record length longer than 128, you must also specify this when you request the BASIC language at start-up time. Respond to the DOS command prompt by entering:

```
BASIC/S:512     or     BASICA/S:512
```

You are asking for the computer's favorite record length, 512 bytes. Your file record will match the physical record.

Writing into a Random Access File

You must perform five tasks when you write a record I/O file. Illustration 14.2, which stores a special name on the disk, shows how these are accomplished.

Task 1: *Set up the I/O Channel.* As with other file types, this is accomplished by line 10. Omitting INPUT, OUTPUT or APPEND tells the computer that random access is to occur and that it will be for either INPUT or OUTPUT. In this illustration, 1 is the number of the channel between the buffer and the file EASY.

Task 2: *Map of the buffer.* The buffer takes the default record size of 128 bytes. The file record is divided into fields and each field assigned to a variable. The FIELD statement in line 20 tells the computer that the buffer for channel 1 will be divided into two fields: one with 15 characters labeled N$; one with 113 bytes labeled D$.

Task 3: *Fill the buffer.* The LSET statements in lines 30 and 40 do this. RUMPELSTILTSKIN is coded into the portion of memory represented by N$. Because of the FIELD statement, this is the first 15 bytes of the buffer. One blank character is assigned to D$, but all of the remaining bytes also become blanks. LSET signifies: left-justify the data in a field and append blanks if necessary. It has a counterpart, the RSET statement, which signifies: right-justify the data and precede them with blanks if the field is not full. If a field is too short, LSET truncates your data at its end; RSET truncates at the beginning.

Task 4: *Copy the contents of the buffer into the file.* The PUT statement in line 50 writes the record in the buffer for channel 1 into the file. (Actually, the computer waits until it has a full sector of data before transfer occurs.) If, as in this example, PUT has no record modifier, the buffer is copied into the disk file record denoted by the current position of the file's pointer. Immediately after the file is opened, this is at the first record of the file. However, after each read or write, the pointer moves to the next record in the file. Because this pointer is invisible and therefore difficult to track, it is a good idea to specify which record you intend to rewrite: change line 50 to something like:

```
50 PUT #1,2
```

This writes RUMPELSTILTSKIN to the second record in the file.

ILLUSTRATION 14.2

Entering a name into a random access file

```
10 OPEN "EASY" AS #1
20 FIELD #1, 15 AS N$, 113 AS D$
30 LSET N$ = "RUMPELSTILTSKIN"
40 LSET D$ = " "
50 PUT #1
60 CLOSE #1
70 END
```

Task 5: *Close the file.* The familiar CLOSE statement in line 60 ends communication between the buffer and the file. It doesn't, however, write out the last buffer filled. Use the PUT statement to do all of the writing you wish to do.

Reading a Random Access File

This involves five equivalent tasks. Illustration 14.3 extracts the name you have written into EASY and displays it on the screen.

Task 1: *Set up the I/O channel.* Use the OPEN statement. Be sure that this OPEN statement matches the one in the file writing program. You need to specify the same file record length each time you use the file.

Task 2: *Map the record in the buffer.* Usually you wish to retrieve information in the same format it had when you wrote it into the file. To do this, use a FIELD statement just like the one you used to set up the file. Here, as in Illustration 14.3, line 20 declares the first 15 bytes to be N$ and the remaining 113 bytes as D$.

Task 3: *Bring the correct record into the buffer.* The GET statement in line 30 brings in the first record of the file because it is executed immediately after the file is opened. Line 30 could include a RECORD modifier. Thus, 30 GET #1,2 would bring the second record into the buffer for you. Fortunately, the RECORD modifier in both the GET and PUT statements can be variables. The record you need can be determined during the program execution and retrieved with lines like:

```
30 GET 1, X
30 GET 1, X+1
```

Task 4: *Use the data in the buffer.* Once it has been copied in, you can use your file data just as any other data in memory. In Illustration 14.3, line 40 prints the contents of N$ on the screen.

Task 5: *Close the file.*

ILLUSTRATION 14.3

Retrieving a name from a random access file

```
10 OPEN "EASY" AS #1
20 FIELD #1, 15 AS N$, 113 AS D$
30 GET #1
40 PRINT N$
50 CLOSE #1
60 END

RUN

RUMPELSTILTSKIN
```

Storing Numbers in Random Access Files

Remember that you must store all information in random access files as character string data. BASIC includes functions which convert numbers to strings and others which reconvert their string representation back to numbers. These conversion functions and their use in the LET statement format are presented in the tables in Illustration 14.4.

The programming examples in Illustration 14.5 write numbers into a random access file and then retrieve and reconvert them for display on the screen.

When numbers are on their way into the file, declare the variables in the FIELD statement to have as many bytes as the type of

ILLUSTRATION 14.4

Number conversion functions

Function	Conversion
N$ = MKI$(N%)	Integer, N%, to 2-byte character string, N$
N$ = MKS$(N!)	Single-precision decimal to 4-byte character string, N$
N$ = MKD$(N#)	Double-precision decimal to 8-byte character string, N$
N% = CVI(N$)	2-Byte character string, N$, to integer, N%
N! = CVS(N$)	4-Byte character string, N$, to single-precision decimal, N!
N# = CVD(N$)	8-Byte character string, N$, to double-precision decimal, N#

number uses. Use the number to be converted (or a variable representing a number) as the argument of the conversion function. When you use the function in a LSET statement, in lines 30, 40, and 50, the converted number will be written into the buffer. PUT copies them out to the disk in this string form.

When numbers come out of the file, your FIELD statement variables must match the type of the number that has been stored. Variables that will represent integers need two bytes, and so on. Once the GET statement copies file data into the buffer, convert the strings to numbers. In Illustration 14.5, the CVI, CVS, and CVD functions in lines 30, 40, and 50 do this. The RUN of this illustration shows that once you do the conversion, PRINT statements display numbers in their usual form.

ILLUSTRATION 14.5

Entering and retrieving numbers from a random access file

Into the file	Out of the file
10 OPEN "NUM" AS #1	10 OPEN "NUM" AS #1
20 FIELD #1,2 AS I$,4 AS S$,8 AS D$	20 FIELD #1, 2 AS I$, 4 AS S$, 8 AS D$
30 LSET I$ = MKI$(8)	30 I% = CVI(I$)
40 LSET S$ = MKS$(8.3)	40 S! = CVS(S$)
50 LSET D$ = MKD$(7.6543217)	50 D# = CVD(D$)
60 PUT #1	60 PRINT I%
70 CLOSE #1	70 PRINT S!
80 END	80 PRINT D#
	90 CLOSE #1
RUN	100 END
OK	RUN
	8
	8.3
	7.6543217
	OK

Updating a Random Access File

Illustration 14.6 is one of the programs that comprise the Computer Dating Project described in Chapter 9. Named CORRECT, its function is to allow you to look at any one record in either the

MALES or FEMALES files, which contain the names and questionnaire responses of all of the participants. The program allows you to select one respondent's record and change the name and responses within it.

Line 50 opens the file specified as S$ in the INPUT statement in line 10. Using variables for file names in OPEN statements adds greatly to the versatility of file maintenance programs such as this one. No LEN= file record length modifier is used because the true dating program file record length depends on the numbers of questions in the questionnaire. Each time the dating project is done, new questionnaires are used; therefore an arbitrary file record length must be set up for the project. A limit of 128 bytes is as good as any, so all of the dating program files must work within this default file record limit.

Line 65 copies into the buffer the record that will be updated. The first task is to display the respondent's name, so line 80 maps the record for the 30-character name, N$, and a dummy, D$, that represents the remaining bytes in the file record. These contain all of the responses to the questionnaire, but they are not needed yet. Line 85 displays the name.

The responses are integers which have been stored in the file as two-byte strings. The FOR . . . NEXT routine in lines 90 through 120 accesses them. It moves the pointer in the buffer through the responses, displaying one at a time. Here a new D$, the dummy, grows with each iteration, representing all of the responses that have previously been displayed. R$ represents the next two bytes of the record, the response that is about to be displayed. PRINT CVI(R$) converts the response to its original numeric form and displays it on the screen.

The remaining lines of this random access file update program accept all new information for the record. The name is rewritten in line 145 and the responses are accepted from the keyboard and rewritten to the buffer one at a time with each iteration of the FOR . . . NEXT loop in lines 150 through 290. PUT #1, F in line 300 guarantees that the newly created record in the buffer will be copied in the same file position as the original.

This example illustrates the key to successful random access file manipulation: keeping track of the invisible pointers. There are two: one for the disk and one for the buffer. The disk file pointer points to the file record currently in use and is controlled by the record number appended to the GET and PUT statements. The buffer pointer aims at the data item or variable currently being

written or read. This is controlled by the length given to each
variable in the FIELD statement.

ILLUSTRATION 14.6

Updating a random access file

```
10 INPUT "MALES OR FEMALES";S$
20 INPUT "HOW MANY PAIRS";P
30 INPUT "HOW MANY QUESTIONS ";Q
40 DIM R(Q)
50 OPEN S$ AS # 1
60 INPUT "ENTER FILE POSITION NUMBER ";F
65 GET # 1,F
70 PRINT "ENTRY  ";F; " IS NOW ";
80 FIELD # 1, 30 AS N$, 98 AS D$
85 PRINT N$
90 FOR  Y = 1 to Q
100     FIELD # 1,30 AS N$, (Y-1)*2 AS D$, 2 AS R$
110     PRINT CVI(R$)
120 NEXT Y
130 PRINT ". . ."
140 INPUT "ENTER CORRECT NAME ";NM$
145 LSET N$ = NM$
150 FOR  Y = 1 TO Q
155     FIELD # 1, 30 AS N$, (Y-1)*2 AS D$, 2 AS R$
160     PRINT "NEW REPLY # ";Y
170     INPUT REPLY(Y)
180     LSET R$ = MKI$(REPLY(Y))
290 NEXT Y
300 PUT # 1, F
310 CLOSE # 1
320 END


RUN

MALES OR FEMALES? MALES
HOW MANY PAIRS? 20
HOW MANY QUESTIONS? 10
ENTER FILE POSITION NUMBER? 1
ENTRY 1 IS NOW BOB
 90
 10
  5
```

```
        6
        3
        3
        8
        2
        9
        2
         .  .  .
ENTER CORRECT NAME? TOM
NEW REPLY # 1
   80
NEW REPLY # 2
   20
NEW REPLY # 3
         .
         .
         .
```

Problems

1. List the number conversion functions used for random access files and explain why you need them.

2. What is the function of the FIELD # statement?

3. What is the difference between the LET statement and the LSET and RSET statements?

4. Think of a file of baseball player statistics where each player's information comprises one file record. Write the BASIC statement to bring the eighth player's stats into the buffer.

Programming problems

5. a. Write a program that allows the accountant in the dentist's office to keep track of the name, number of cavities, and amount owed for each patient. Use a random access file that stores the information for each patient in one file record. Run the program and enter sample data for a few patients.

   b. Write a program that allows the accountant to enter a patient's ID number, and have the computer select that record and print how much money the patient owes. The ID number and the file record number will match. Have the computer accept a payment amount and update the patient's file record to reflect the payment.

6. a. Write a record I/O file that contains sequential floating-point values of 1.0 to 512.0.
   b. Show that you have succeeded.
   c. Modify the file to replace the entries 70, 234, and 300 with the words SKILLERY, SKALLERY, and ALIGATOR respectively.
   d. Show that you have succeeded.

7. a. Store the name and ID number of each employee of the Central Bank in a random access file.
   b. Use the computer to allow the security guard to check workers as they arrive. When the guard enters the employee's name, have the computer print the matching ID number.

8. Use the computer to keep track of the inventory of ladies' shoes for the Cinderella Shoe Company. In a random access file, store the style number and the quantity on hand for each style. There are 64 styles numbered from 1001 to 1064. Follow the steps below:
   a. Begin by putting initial quantity values in the file for each style.
   b. Tie the file into a cash register that subtracts from the quantity on hand each time a pair of shoes is sold.
   c. Print out an inventory list that shows the style and quantity on hand.

9. You are an official of the United States Olympic Committee. The Winter Olympics are finished and the data have been stored in a random access file. Your job is to read the data about the medal winners and print out a chart like this one:

```
MEN'S DOWNHILL SKIING


GOLD: IGGY PIGGY              USA
SILVER: OLAF TOLSTOY          USSR
BRONZE: ALFRED MINCINI        ITAL
```

and so forth for all six Olympic events. Allow 26 bytes for the name of each event and 30 bytes for the names of each winner and 4 bytes for the initials of the winner's country. Write a program so that historians may inquire about any single event and see the gold, silver, and bronze medal winners. Break the project into three parts:

   a. Write a program to enter the names of the medalists and their countries for each event.
   b. Write a program to print out a list of each event with the name and country of each medalist.
   c. Write a program that allows historians to inquire about any one event.

10. Use a record I/O file to store bibliographic information on articles in the library concerning computers. In block 1, set up an index that points to the rest of the file. In the blocks that follow the index, use 64-byte file records to store the full bibliographic information for each article. Allow for 8 articles. Each index notation requires a title for an article that is abbreviated to 12 characters, and two integer numbers that refer to the block location — and the file record location within the block — of the full bibliographic description of the article. Write four programs:

a. Initialize and pre-extend the file. You may want to set up in advance the block and file record pointers for each index entry.

b. Ask the librarian for the abbreviated title of the article and store it in the index. Then accept the full bibliographic description of the article and store that in the appropriate block of the file.

c. Print out the index and the full bibliographic notation for every article in the index.

d. Let the librarian look up information about any one of the index entries.

Appendix

Operating Instructions
for the Dating Program

1. The dating program is a network of five BASIC programs
   that serve to:
   a. provide a menu of related programs.
   b. enter data into a males file named MALES and a females
      file named FEMALES.
   c. check the data in either file.
   d. correct the data in either file.
   e. create ideal matches between males and females.
   The programs for steps a through d make up the Appendix.
   The program that creates ideal matches is listed in Chapter 9.

2. As a user of the dating program you must:
   a. develop a questionnaire.
   b. collect responses from *equal* numbers of males and
      females.
   c. insert the Dating Program diskette into an IBM personal
      computer.
   d. enter RUN "MENU", and select each option in sequence.

3. The questionnaire.
   a. See the sample questionnaire in Illustration 9.7. Make
      yours similar in having the first two questions answered
      as percentages which add up to 100. These should tell

what emphasis the respondent places on material things and what emphasis the respondent places on interpersonal relations.

b. Keep the questionnaire short. The computer analyzes each answer carefully and checks each male against each female. The process may take a while.

c. The answers to questions (other than questions 1 and 2) should be a one-digit number from 0 to 9.

4. Entering replies.
   a. Type RUN "MENU".
   b. Choose option 1 on the menu. Enter all of the males into the MALES file at once and all of the females into FEMALES.
   c. Enter the person's name as you wish it to be printed in the final roster of partners.
   d. Answers 1 and 2 are two-digit whole numbers that represent percentages. All others are one digit.

5. Checking replies.
   a. Choose option 2 on the menu. Enter the file name (MALES or FEMALES) and watch the contents of the file on the display. If it scrolls by too fast, press CTRL and NUM-LOCK and the screen will halt. Press any key and the scroll will continue.
   b. If you see an entry you wish to correct, make note of its place in the file. You will change all of the data for one person even if you only wish to correct one aspect of his or her file data.

6. Making corrections.
   a. Choose option 3 on the menu. Enter the name of the file that contains the data to be corrected.
   b. Enter the place of the entry in its file. (The third person in the file has place number 3 and so on.)
   c. The computer will show the data of that entry as it is currently stored by the computer. Then, it will prompt you to re-enter all of the file data for that person. Your new entries will replace the previous file data.

7. Selecting partners.
   a. Once all of the file data for the males and females is correct, choose option 4 on the menu.

b. The display will indicate that the Dating Program is working, and the computer will process the responses given by each person and compare them with the responses given by all of the others who are of the opposite sex. Finally, it will begin printing on the printer the roster of ideal partners. *Option 5 may take several hours.* Plan ahead! Set it running early in the day and collect your matches at the day's end. Using a 10-question questionnaire to match 50 couples takes the computer about 30 minutes.

8. Finishing up.
   When you no longer need your file data, clear the MALES and FEMALES files by giving the KILL "MALES" and KILL "FEMALES" command.

Auxiliary Programs for the Computer Dating Project

The programs that follow must be stored on the Dating Program diskette. When the diskette has been booted, enter RUN "MENU" and follow the sequence of options.

1. The program named MENU

```
10 CLS
20 PRINT TAB(28);"PARTNER MATCHING MENU"
30 PRINT:PRINT
40 PRINT TAB(30);"1. ENTER REPLIES"
50 PRINT TAB(30);"2. CHECK REPLIES"
60 PRINT TAB(30);"3. CORRECT REPLIES"
70 PRINT TAB(30);"4. SELECT PARTNERS"
80 PRINT TAB(30);"5. STOP"
90 PRINT:PRINT
100 INPUT "ENTER OPTION NUMBER";N
110 ON N GOTO 120,130,140,150,160
120 RUN "ENTER"
130 RUN "CHECK"
140 RUN "CORRECT"
150 RUN "DATING"
160 PRINT:PRINT:PRINT
170 CLS
180 END
```

2. The program named ENTER

```
7 PRINT TAB(20);"ENTER DATA FOR PARTNER
MATCHING":PRINT:PRINT
10 INPUT "MALES OR FEMALES";S$
20 INPUT "HOW MANY PAIRS";P
30 INPUT "HOW MANY QUESTIONS";Q
40 OPEN S$ AS 1
50 FOR X = 1 TO P
60     FIELD 1,30 AS N$,2*Q AS D$
70     PRINT "NAME ";X
75     INPUT NM$
80     LSET N$ = NM$
85     FOR Y = 1 TO Q
90         FIELD 1,30 AS N$,(Y-1)*2 AS D$,2 AS R$
100        PRINT "REPLY #";Y
110        INPUT REPLY(Y)
115        LSET R$ = MKI$(REPLY(Y))
120    NEXT Y
130    PUT 1
140 NEXT X
150 CLOSE 1
160 RUN "MENU"
170 END
```

3. The program named CHECK

```
7 PRINT TAB(20);"CHECK DATA FOR PARTNER MATCHING"
8 PRINT:PRINT
10 INPUT "MALES OR FEMALES";S$
20 INPUT "HOW MANY PAIRS";P
30 INPUT "HOW MANY QUESTIONS";Q
40 OPEN S$ AS 1
50 FOR X = 1 TO P
55     GET 1
60     FIELD 1,30 AS N$,2*Q AS D$
65     PRINT S$;" NO.";X
70     PRINT N$
80     FOR Y = 1 TO Q
90         FIELD 1,30 AS N$,(Y-1)*2 AS D$,2 AS R$
100        PRINT CVI(R$)
120    NEXT Y
130    PRINT ". . ."
```

```
135 FOR Y = 1 TO 700
136 NEXT Y
140 NEXT X
150 CLOSE 1
160 RUN "MENU"
170 END
```

4. The program named CORRECT

```
5 CLS
7 PRINT TAB(20);"CORRECT DATA FOR PARTNER
MATCHING":PRINT:PRINT
10 INPUT "MALES OR FEMALES";S$
20 INPUT "HOW MANY PAIRS";P
30 INPUT "HOW MANY QUESTIONS ";Q
40 DIM R(Q)
50 OPEN S$ AS 1
60 INPUT "ENTER FILE POSITION NUMBER ";F
65 GET 1,F
70 PRINT "ENTRY ";F;" IS NOW ";
80 FIELD 1,30 AS N$, 98 AS D$
85 PRINT N$
90 FOR Y = 1 TO Q
100    FIELD 1,30 AS N$, (Y-1)*2 AS D$,2 AS R$
110    PRINT CVI(R$)
120 NEXT Y
130 PRINT ". . ."
140 INPUT "ENTER CORRECT NAME ";NM$
145 LSET N$ = NM$
150 FOR Y = 1 TO Q
155    FIELD 1, 30 AS N$, (Y-1)*2 AS D$, 2 AS R$
160    PRINT "NEW REPLY # ";Y
170    INPUT REPLY(Y)
180    LSET R$ = MKI$(REPLY(Y))
290 NEXT Y
300 PUT 1, F
310 CLOSE 1
320 RUN "MENU"
330 END
```

5. The program named DATING

The program named DATING completes the series of programs for the Computer Dating Project and is listed in Chapter 9.

Answers to Selected Problems

Chapter 1

1. a. NEW
   b. LIST
   c. LLIST
   d. RUN

2. NEW

```
10 PRINT "THE BROOKLYN BRIDGE"
20 PRINT "STARTED IN 1870 AND FINISHED IN 1883"
25 PRINT "WORK WAS DANGEROUS AND SLOW"
30 PRINT "IT TOOK"
40 PRINT 1883-1870
50 PRINT "YEARS TO BUILD"
60 END

10 PRINT "THE GEORGE WASHINGTON BRIDGE"
20 PRINT "STARTED IN 1927 AND FINISHED IN 1931"
40 PRINT 1931-1927

RUN

THE GEORGE WASHINGTON BRIDGE
STARTED IN 1927 AND FINISHED IN 1931
WORK WAS DANGEROUS AND SLOW
IT TOOK
 4
YEARS TO BUILD
```

4. NEW

```
10 PRINT "THE AGE OF MICKEY MOUSE WAS:"
20 PRINT 1969-1929
30 PRINT "WHEN I WAS BORN"
40 END

RUN

THE AGE OF MICKEY MOUSE WAS:
 40
WHEN I WAS BORN
```

10. a. Correct
   b. 55 PRINT X; "IS THE SOLUTION"
   c. 28 PRINT Y; "IS NOT THE SOLUTION"
   d. Correct
   e. 5 PRINT "YOUR AGE"

Chapter 2

1. Left-hand column

```
 87 = 1010111
 63 = 111111
100 = 1100100
 17 = 10001
 77 = 1001101
  5 = 101
  3 = 11
  6 = 110
 16 = 10000
 86 = 1010110
 65 = 1000001
 75 = 1001011
```

2. Left-hand column

```
100101   =  37
1000111  =  71
10111    =  23
10100    =  20
1111     =  15
1110     =  14
1010011  =  83
110011   =  51
1011100  =  92
1101111  = 111
11000000 = 192
10000111 = 135
1000100  =  68
10010010 = 146
1100000  =  96
```

10. a. The need to store vast amounts of data has produced computer disk, tape, and other storage devices.
    b. The search for a fast calculating machine has produced the central processing unit (CPU).
    c. The desire to do these things automatically has led to the stored computer program.
11. Binary digits can be represented electrically; a closed circuit that is ON represents a ONE and an open circuit that is OFF represents ZERO. Collections of binary digits form codes that represent human readable characters and numbers. As a result, human concepts are represented, stored, and processed electronically in computer systems.
12. The bytes used to store a number determine two things:
    a. The number of significant digits that can be retained (the precision of the computer's numbers)
    b. The range of numbers that can be represented (the magnitude of the computer's numbers)
13. After the OK prompt enter:

```
FILES
```

You will see columns with names of system and user programs:

```
COMMAND.COM FORMAT. COM CHKDSK .COM SYS     .COM
   .           .          .          .         .
   .           .          .          .         .
   .           .          .          .         .
AGE     .BAS PURRKY. BAS TIME    .BAS LOTTER .BAS
OK
```

Select one and run it:

```
RUN "PURRKY"
YOU NEED A 21.19 FOOT LONG LADDER
OK
```

Chapter 3

1. a. 90 READ A
   b. 74 DATA 88
   c. 30 INPUT A,B,C
   d. Correct
   e. 40 DATA 45, 9, 3, 2.6, 12, 5
   f. Correct
   g. Correct
   h. 58 INPUT A
   i. 20 READ N$, A$, P$
   j. Correct
   k. 77 PRINT "ENTER YOUR NAME"
   l. 5 LET N$ = "SUZY"

3. a. Correct
   b. Syntax error in 20 (can't read alphanumeric data with number variables)
   c. Out-of-data in 10

4. a. Line 20 should be a DATA statement.
   b. Yes, but it's silly because CAT is never read.
   c. Yes.

7. IS
   MELANIE
   21
   MELANIE IS 21

11. 10 LET P = 2*2
    20 LET A = 2*25
    30 LET C = 2*35
    40 LET I = 2*8
    50 PRINT "PERCENT OF NUTRIENTS STILL NEEDED TODAY."
    55 PRINT
    60 PRINT "PROTEIN", 100-P
    70 PRINT "VITAMIN A", 100-A
    90 PRINT "VITAMIN C", 100-C
    100 PRINT "IRON", 100-I
    110 END

    RUN

    PERCENT OF NUTRIENTS STILL NEEDED TODAY.

    PROTEIN   96
    VITAMIN A   50
    VITAMIN C   30
    IRON   84

14. 10 INPUT "HELLO TELL ME YOUR NAME, PLEASE"; Q$
    20 PRINT "LET'S HAVE SOME FUN ";Q$
    30 PRINT "TYPE IN A NOUN, A VERB, AN ADVERB, AND AN ADJECTIVE."
    40 INPUT N$,V$,A$,J$
    50 PRINT "THE ENORMOUS ";N$;" IS ALWAYS ";J$;
    60 PRINT " EVEN WHEN IT ";V$;" AFTER THE COOK TALKS ";A$;"."
    70 END

    RUN

    HELLO TELL ME YOUR NAME, PLEASE? MARTHA
    LET'S HAVE SOME FUN MARTHA
    TYPE IN A NOUN, A VERB, AN ADVERB, AND AN ADJECTIVE.
    ? HORSE
    ? CHEWS
    ? ROUGHLY
    ? GREASY
    THE ENORMOUS HORSE IS ALWAYS GREASY
    EVEN WHEN IT CHEWS AFTER THE COOK TALKS ROUGHLY.

15. 10 READ A$,A,B,C,
    20 READ B$,D,E,F

```
30 READ C$,G,H,I
40 READ D$,J,K,L
50 READ E$,M,N,O
55 LET S = A+B+C+D+E+F+G+H+I+J+K+L+M+N+O
60 PRINT "NAME","TOTAL POINTS"
70 PRINT
80 PRINT A$,A+B+C
90 PRINT B$,D+E+F
100 PRINT C$,G+H+I
110 PRINT D$,J+K+L
120 PRINT E$,M+N+O
130 PRINT
140 PRINT "TOTAL POINTS FOR THE TEAM:";S
150 DATA MARVIN,1,0,0
160 DATA PETER,2,2,1
180 DATA FRED,1,1,1
190 DATA ALAN,2,0,1
200 DATA BILL,0,1,1
210 END

RUN

NAME        TOTAL POINTS

MARVIN        1
PETER         5
FRED          3
ALAN          3
BILL          2

TOTAL POINTS FOR THE TEAM: 14
```

Chapter 4

1. a. $(4^2 \times 2^3)^{.5} = \sqrt{4^2 \times 2^3} = \sqrt{128}$

   b. $\dfrac{22}{2} \times 4 + 11 - \dfrac{3^2}{.3} = 25$

   c. $\dfrac{\left(\dfrac{.3}{.9} \times 3 - 9\right)}{3} = -2.67$

2. a. `10 PRINT (2+4^2)/(5*8)`
   b. `10 PRINT (3+9)/8-4*2/2^2`
   c. `10 PRINT 3*(6.2+5)/(4.5-2.3)`
   d. `10 PRINT 10*SQR(25+11)`
3. a. `30 PRINT 5*3/2`
   b. `33 PRINT "ANSWER"; INT(X+.5)`
   c. `12 PRINT (3*X)+4*Y+Z^2`
   d. `37 PRINT "X = C", "A = X^2","B = X^3"`
   e. Correct

    f. `100 PRINT INT(150.75)`
    g. Correct
    h. `60 RANDOMIZE`
    i. `67 RANDOMIZE X`
    j. Correct

8.
```
20 INPUT "ENTER THE PRICE"; P
30 V = INT(P)
40 C = P-V
50 PRINT "THE BOOKSTORE GETS";V;"DOLLARS"
60 PRINT "CHILDREN'S CHARITY GETS";C;"CENTS"
70 PRINT
80 GO TO 20
90 END

Ready

RUN

ENTER THE PRICE? 12.45
THE BOOKSTORE GETS 12 DOLLARS
CHILDREN'S CHARITY GETS .45 CENTS

ENTER THE PRICE? 2.85
THE BOOKSTORE GETS 2 DOLLARS
CHILDREN'S CHARITY GETS .85 CENTS

ENTER THE PRICE? CTRL//BREAK
```

11.
```
5 RANDOMIZE 128
10 J = INT(RND*100)+1
20 A = INT(RND*(200-101+1)+101)
30 S = INT(RND*(250-201+1)+201)
40 PRINT "JUVENILE WINNER:";J
50 PRINT "ADULT WINNER:   ";A
60 PRINT "SENIOR WINNER:  ";S
70 END

RUN

JUVENILE WINNER: 53
ADULT WINNER:    116
SENIOR WINNER:   211
```

Chapter 5

3. a. `67 NEXT X`
    b. Correct
    c. Correct if B is negative
    d. Correct

e. 56 IF A = B THEN 120
f. 71 IF INT(X) = 2 THEN 55
g. 30 FOR B = 100 TO C STEP −5
h. Correct
i. Correct
j. Correct

4. a. 30 FOR P = 100 TO 1 STEP−2
   b. 70 IF A$ = 'HUNTINGTON" THEN 80
   c. Correct
   d. Correct
   e. 22 IF A$ = "YES" THEN 100
   f. 60 IF G$ = "234" THEN 100
   g. Correct
   h. WEND
   i. Correct
   j. WEND

5. ?2 (user's choice)
   THUNDER

   THUNDER
   SUNSHINE
   LIGHTNING

6. HALLOWEEN
   PUMPKINS

7. 1
   5
   5
   9
   9
   13
   13
   17
   17
   21

12. HELLO
    HELLO
    HELLO
    HELLO
    GOODBYE

13. 1
    2
    3
    4
    5
    6
    7

```
            8
            9
           10
```

14.
```
     1    1
     1    2
     1    3
     1    4
     2    1
     2    2
     2    3
     2    4
```

23. Zeros will be printed forever. The value of X never changes, so the loop will never stop.

24.
```
COURSE: MATH
ENROLLMENT: 23
COURSE: ENG
ENROLLMENT: 20
COURSE: HIST
ENROLLMENT: 18
```

27.
```
10 PRINT "WHAT IS YOUR AGE";
20 INPUT A
30 IF A > = 18 THEN 100
40 PRINT "YOU MUST WAIT ";18-A;"YEARS TO VOTE."
50 GO TO 120
100 PRINT "YOU MAY VOTE."
120 END

RUN

WHAT IS YOUR AGE? 12
YOU MUST WAIT 6 YEARS TO VOTE.

RUN

WHAT IS YOUR AGE? 19
YOU MAY VOTE.
```

28.
```
10 FOR X = 1 TO 9
20 PRINT "WHAT IS";X;"TIMES 9";
30 INPUT G
40 IF G = X*9 THEN 100
50 PRINT "WRONG"
60 GO TO 110
100 PRINT "CORRECT"
105 C = C+1
110 NEXT X
120 PRINT "YOU GOT ";C;"CORRECT"
130 END
```

```
        RUN

        WHAT IS 1 TIMES 9? 9
        CORRECT
        WHAT IS 2 TIMES 9? 25
        WRONG
        WHAT IS 3 TIMES 9? 27
        CORRECT
        WHAT IS 4 TIMES 9? 36
        CORRECT
        WHAT IS 5 TIMES 9? 20
        WRONG
        WHAT IS 6 TIMES 9? 54
        CORRECT
        WHAT IS 7 TIMES 9? 63
        CORRECT
        WHAT IS 8 TIMES 9? 75
        WRONG
        WHAT IS 9 TIMES 9? 81
        CORRECT
        YOU GOT 6 CORRECT
```

34.
```
    10 FOR Z = 1 TO 5
    20 READ Q$,A$
    30 PRINT Q$
    40 INPUT G$
    50 IF G$ = A$ THEN 100
    60 PRINT "SORRY, YOU'RE WRONG"
    70 GO TO 110
    100 PRINT "VERY GOOD"
    105 E = E+1
    110 NEXT Z
    120 PRINT
    130 PRINT "YOU GOT";E;"OUT OF 5 CORRECT."
    140 DATA "WHO PLAYS BASEBALL IN MONTREAL",EXPOS
    150 DATA "WHO PLAYS BASEBALL IN BOSTON",RED SOX
    160 DATA "WHO PLAYS BASEBALL IN LOS ANGELES", DODGERS
    170 DATA "WHO PLAYS BASEBALL IN SAN FRANCISCO",GIANTS
    180 DATA "WHO PLAYS BASEBALL IN PITTSBURGH",PIRATES
    190 END

    RUN

    WHO PLAYS BASEBALL IN MONTREAL
    ? EXPOS
    VERY GOOD
    WHO PLAYS BASEBALL IN BOSTON
    ? COWBOYS
    SORRY, YOU'RE WRONG
    WHO PLAYS BASEBALL IN LOS ANGELES
    ? GIANTS
    SORRY, YOU'RE WRONG
```

```
WHO PLAYS BASEBALL IN SAN FRANCISCO
? GIANTS
VERY GOOD
WHO PLAYS BASEBALL IN PITTSBURGH
? PIRATES
VERY GOOD
YOU GOT 3 OUT OF 5 CORRECT.
```

35.
```
10  WHILE Q$ < > "MAINE"
20     READ Q$,A$
30     PRINT "WHAT IS THE CAPITAL OF ";Q$
40     INPUT G$
50     IF A$ = G$ THEN PRINT "RIGHT" ELSE PRINT "WRONG"
60  WEND
70  DATA KANSAS, TOPEKA, OREGON, SALEM, MAINE, AUGUSTA
80  END

RUN

WHAT IS THE CAPITAL OF KANSAS
? TOPEKA
RIGHT
WHAT IS THE CAPITAL OF OREGON
? PORTLAND
WRONG
WHAT IS THE CAPITAL OF MAINE
? PORTLAND
WRONG
```

Chapter 6

1. a. Correct
   b. Correct
   c. Correct
   d. Correct
   e. Correct
   f. 34 A(Y) = INT(10*R+1)

7.
```
10 RANDOMIZE 999
20 DIM N$(10)
30 DIM C(3)
40 FOR X = 1 TO 10
50     READ N$(X)
60 NEXT X
70 FOR Y = 1 TO 3
```

```
80       R = INT(RND*10+1)
90       FOR X = 1 TO Y-1
100             IF R = C(X) THEN 80
110      NEXT X
120      C(Y) = R
130 NEXT Y
140 PRINT "THE COLORS FOR TODAY ARE:"
150 FOR X = 1 TO 3
160      PRINT N$(C(X))
170 NEXT X
180 DATA RED,BLUE,GREEN,YELLOW,ORANGE
190 DATA WHITE,PINK,PURPLE,BLACK,BROWN
200 END

RUN

THE COLORS FOR TODAY ARE:
RED
WHITE
YELLOW
```

8.
```
10 DIM W(5,5)
15 DIM D$(5)
20 FOR X = 1 TO 5
30      READ D$(X)
40      PRINT D$(X):PRINT
50      FOR Y = 1 TO 5
60            PRINT "ENTER NUMBER OF BOXES FOR EMPLOYEE #";Y
62            INPUT W(X,Y)
65            T = T+W(X,Y)
70      NEXT Y
80 NEXT X
90 FOR X = 1 TO 5
100     FOR Y = 1 TO 5
110           IF W(X,Y) <= H THEN 120
115           H = W(X,Y)
117           P = Y
119           D = X
120     NEXT Y
130 NEXT X
150 PRINT
160 PRINT "THE AVERAGE OF BOXES PACKED THIS WEEK IS";T/25
170 PRINT "THE MOST PACKED BY ONE PERSON WAS";H
175 PRINT "IT WAS PACKED BY EMPLOYEE #";P
176 PRINT "ON ";D$(D)
180 PRINT "KEEP IT UP!!"
190 DATA MONDAY,TUESDAY,WEDNESDAY,THURSDAY,FRIDAY
200 END
```

```
RUN
  .
  .
  .
ENTER NUMBER OF BOXES FOR EMPLOYEE # 5
? 28
FRIDAY

ENTER NUMBER OF BOXES FOR EMPLOYEE # 1
? 12
ENTER NUMBER OF BOXES FOR EMPLOYEE # 2
? 18
ENTER NUMBER OF BOXES FOR EMPLOYEE # 3
? 30
ENTER NUMBER OF BOXES FOR EMPLOYEE # 4
? 26
ENTER NUMBER OF BOXES FOR EMPLOYEE # 5
? 25

THE AVERAGE OF BOXES PACKED THIS WEEK IS 25.52
THE MOST PACKED BY ONE PERSON WAS 45
IT WAS PACKED BY EMPLOYEE # 2
ON WEDNESDAY
KEEP IT UP!!
```

9. 5 DIM T$(2,5)   (Two teams and five wrestlers each as an example)
```
10 DIM W(2,5)
12 DIM S$(5),X$(5)
20 FOR X = 1 TO 2
30     FOR Y = 1 to 5
40         INPUT T$(X,Y)
45         INPUT W(X,Y)
50     NEXT Y
60 NEXT X
68 C = 1
69 REM H STARTS WITH HIGHEST POINTS POSSIBLE
70 FOR H = 100 TO 0 STEP -1
80     FOR X = 1 TO 2
90         FOR Y = 1 TO 5
100            IF W(X,Y) <> H THEN 210
150            S$(C) = T$(X,Y)
160            ON X GO TO 170, 180
170            X$(C) = "NORTH HIGH"
175            GO TO 190
180            X$(C) = "SOUTH HIGH"
190            C = C+1
200            IF C > 5 THEN 250
210        NEXT Y
220    NEXT X
230 NEXT H
250 PRINT "THE TOP FIVE WRESTLERS ARE"
260 PRINT
```

```
270 FOR X = 1 TO 5
280     PRINT S$(X);" FROM ";X$(X)
290 NEXT X
300 END

RUN

? AWFUL FIGHTER
? 29
? INCREDIBLY STRONG
? 45
? TERRIBLY TOUGH
? 89
? OUTRAGEOUS OUCH
? 70
? SPECTACULAR SPEED
? 10
? TINY TOUGH
? 1
? LITTLE MEAN
? 22
? SWEETIE PIE
? 66
? HONEY BUNCH
? 75
? SUGAR BABY
? 33

THE TOP FIVE WRESTLERS ARE

TERRIBLY TOUGH FROM NORTH HIGH
HONEY BUNCH FROM SOUTH HIGH
OUTRAGEOUS OUCH FROM NORTH HIGH
SWEETIE PIE FROM SOUTH HIGH
INCREDIBLY STRONG FROM NORTH HIGH
```

Chapter 7

1. a. Correct
   b. 12 DEF FNP(M) = M*7
   c. Correct
   d. 22 DEF FNA(X) = X^2
   e. 98 GO SUB 100
   f. 66 DEF FNA(X) = 9/X
   g. Correct
   h. 71 DEF FNB(A,B,C) = A*B*C
   i. 6675 DEF FNP(X) =X^2−2*X+1
   j. 15 DEF FNS(X) = Y*X

4. X   FNP(X)
   1   −2

```
          2    -1
          3     2
          4     7
          5    14

5. 1 RANDOMIZE 123
   5 C = 0
   10 FOR X = 1 TO 12
   20    FOR Y = 1 TO 12
   25       W = 0
   30       PRINT "WHAT IS";Y;"TIMES";X
   35       INPUT G
   40       IF G = Y*X THEN GO SUB 150:PRINT A$:GO TO 105
   42       IF W = 1 THEN GO SUB 200:PRINT A$:GO TO 110
   45       W = W + 1 (only two tries)
   50       PRINT "TRY AGAIN"
   55       GO TO 30
   105      C = C + 1
   110   NEXT Y
   115 PRINT
   120 NEXT X
   130 INPUT "YOU GOT";C;"CORRECT"
   135 GO TO 999
   150 R = INT(5*RND + 1)
   160 FOR I = 1 TO R
   170    READ A$
   180 NEXT I
   190 RESTORE
   195 RETURN
   200 R = INT(5*RND + 1)
   210 FOR I = 1 TO 5+R
   220    READ A$
   230 NEXT I
   240 RESTORE
   250 RETURN
   300 DATA CORRECT,FINE,GOOD,SWELL!,WOW!
   310 DATA SORRY,BAD!,NOPE,NO,BOOO
   999 END

   RUN

   WHAT IS 1 TIMES 1
   ? 1
   SWELL!
   WHAT IS 2 TIMES 1
   ? 14
   BOOO
   .
   .
   .

   YOU GOT 9 CORRECT

9. 1000 IF ERR<>6 THEN ON ERROR GO TO 0
```

```
       1010 PRINT "NUMBER TOO LARGE"
       1020 RESUME
```

10. ```
    10 ON ERROR GO TO 500
       .
       .
       .
    400 READ X,Y,A,B,C
       .
       .
    450 DATA 2,4,5,6
       .
       .
       .
    500 IF ERR<>4 THEN ON ERROR GO TO 0
    510 PRINT "CHECK YOUR DATA LIST"
    520 RESUME 530
    530 END
    ```

Chapter 8

1. f. 48 IF LEN(A$) = 16 THEN 100
   g. 23 T$ = LEFT$(V$,3)
   h. 56 M$ = MID$(F$,2,4)
   i. 23 IF VAL(X$) = 495 THEN 56
   j. 55 D$ = LEN(V$)

2. PA
   ME
   ROME
   10

6. ```
   5 C = 1
   10 INPUT A$
   20 FOR X = 1 TO 80
   30    IF MID$(A$,X,1) = " " THEN C = C + 1
   40    IF MID$(A$,X,1) = "." THEN 100
   50 NEXT X
   100 PRINT "THERE WERE ";C;" WORDS IN THE SENTENCE."
   120 END

   RUN

   ? COMPUTERS ARE INCREDIBLE.
   THERE WERE 3 WORDS IN THE SENTENCE.
   ```

11. ```
    10 PRINT "ENTER THE STATISTICS WITH 8 DIGITS AS FOLLOWS"
    20 PRINT "    2 DIGITS HOME TEAM'S SCORE"
    30 PRINT "    2 DIGITS VISITORS' SCORE"
    40 PRINT "    1 DIGIT QUARTER BEING PLAYED"
    50 PRINT "    1 DIGIT DOWN BEING PLAYED"
    ```
    ```

```
60 PRINT "   2 DIGITS YARDS"
70 INPUT S$
80 H$ = LEFT$(S$,2)
90 V$ = MID$(S$,3,2)
100 Q$ = MID$(S$,5,1)
110 D$ = MID$(S$,6,1)
120 Y$ = RIGHT$(S$,2)
130 PRINT:PRINT:PRINT
140 PRINT"_____"
150 PRINT"          SCOREBOARD                    "
160 PRINT
170 PRINT
180 PRINT" HOME     VISITORS     QUARTER    DOWN      YARDS "
190 PRINT    TAB(2);H$;TAB(10);V$;TAB(25);Q$;TAB(35); D$;TAB(50);Y$
200 PRINT
210 PRINT
220 PRINT"_____"
230 END

RUN

ENTER THE STATISTICS WITH 8 DIGITS AS FOLLOWS
     2 DIGITS HOME TEAM'S SCORE
     2 DIGITS VISITORS' SCORE
     1 DIGIT QUARTER BEING PLAYED
     1 DIGIT DOWN BEING PLAYED
     2 DIGITS YARDS
? 07141308
```

	SCOREBOARD			
HOME	VISITORS	QUARTER	DOWN	YARDS
07	14	1	3	08

```
12. 10 REM THIS IS A STUDY OF NUTRITION
    20 V$ = " \      \  ###.#"
    30 READ P,A,C,I
    20 P = P*1.5
    30 A = A*1.5
    40 C = C*1.5
    50 I = I*1.5
    60 PRINT "OUNCES REQUIRED TO GROW"
    70 PRINT USING V$;"PROTEIN",P
    80 PRINT USING V$;"VIT. A", A
    90 PRINT USING V$;"VIT. C", C
    100 PRINT USING V$;"IRON", I
    110 DATA 2, 10, 15, 9
    120 END

    RUN

    OUNCES REQUIRED TO GROW
    PROTEIN   3.0
```

```
VIT. A 15.0
VIT. C 22.5
IRON   13.5
```

Chapter 9

1.

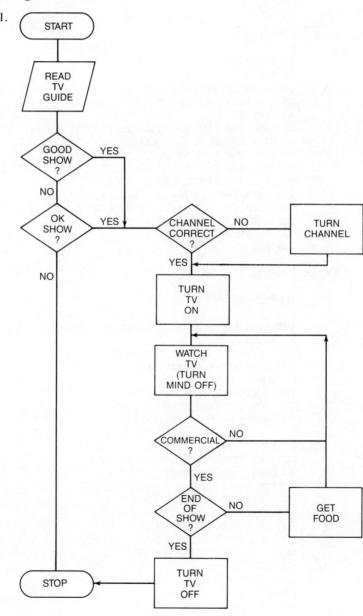

Chapter 12

1. the RAM.
4. the smallest number of bytes that is transferred to or from a file. On the IBM personal computer a physical record has 512 bytes.
5. all of the information pertaining to one unit in a file. (File records are usually divided into fields. Usually several file records fit into one physical record.)

Chapter 13

5a.
```
10 OPEN "JEWELS" FOR OUTPUT AS #1
20 FOR X = 1 TO 8
30    READ N$,S$,C$
35    PRINT #1,N$;",";S$;",";C$
40 NEXT X
50 DATA THE PINK BOUTIQUE,MILLBROOKE,P
60 DATA ROTHBURN'S,ASHLEY,G
70 DATA THE SPOTTED TORTOISE,ATHENS,G
80 DATA THE IRON HORSE,MILWAUKEE,P
90 DATA SHIRLEY'S,ROME,G
100 DATA THE BUTTERFLY SHOP,HAMILTON,G
110 DATA THE JEWELRY SHOP,MILLVILLE,G
120 DATA THE HOBBY HORSE,FRANKLIN,P
130 CLOSE #1
140 END
```

5a. Results:

```
JEWELS

THE PINK BOUTIQUE,MILLBROOKE,P
ROTHBURN'S,ASHLEY,G
THE SPOTTED TORTOISE,ATHENS,G
THE IRON HORSE,MILWAUKEE,P
SHIRLEY'S,ROME,G
THE BUTTERFLY SHOP,HAMILTON,G
THE JEWELRY SHOP,MILLVILLE,G
THE HOBBY HORSE,FRANKLIN,P
```

5b.
```
10 OPEN "JEWELS" FOR INPUT AS #1
20 OPEN "POOR" FOR OUTPUT AS #2
30 OPEN "GOOD" FOR OUTPUT AS #3
40 FOR X = 1 TO 8
50    INPUT #1,N$,S$,C$
60    IF C$ = "P" THEN 90
70    PRINT #3,N$;",";S$
80    GOTO 100
90    PRINT #2,N$;",";S$
100 NEXT X
110 CLOSE #1,#2,#3
120 END
```

5b. Results:

```
GOOD.DAT

ROTHBURN'S,ASHLEY
THE SPOTTED TORTOISE,ATHENS
SHIRLEY'S,ROME
THE BUTTERFLY SHOP,HAMILTON
THE JEWELRY SHOP,MILLVILLE


POOR.DAT

THE PINK BOUTIQUE,MILLBROOKE
THE IRON HORSE,MILWAUKEE
THE HOBBY HORSE,FRANKLIN
```

5c.
```
10 ON ERROR GOTO 500
20 INPUT "WHICH LIST DO YOU WISH TO SEE";L$
30 IF L$ = "POOR" THEN 100
40 OPEN "GOOD" FOR INPUT AS #1
45 PRINT
50 PRINT TAB(15);"THE GOOD CREDIT LIST"
60 PRINT
70 GOTO 200
100 OPEN "POOR" FOR INPUT AS # 1
110 PRINT
120 PRINT TAB(15);"THE POOR CREDIT LIST"
130 PRINT
200 INPUT #1,N$,S$
210 PRINT TAB(10);N$;TAB(35);S$
220 GOTO 200
500 IF ERR <> 62 THEN ON ERROR GOTO 0
510 RESUME 530
530 CLOSE #1
540 END

RUN

WHICH LIST DO YOU WISH TO SEE? POOR

           THE POOR CREDIT LIST

     THE PINK BOUTIQUE     MILLBROOKE
     THE IRON HORSE        MILWAUKEE
     THE HOBBY HORSE       FRANKLIN

RUN

WHICH LIST DO YOU WISH TO SEE? GOOD

           THE GOOD CREDIT LIST
```

```
ROTHBURN'S            ASHLEY
THE SPOTTED TORTOISE  ATHENS
SHIRLEY'S             ROME
THE BUTTERFLY SHOP    HAMILTON
THE JEWELRY SHOP      MILLVILLE
```

7a.
```
10 OPEN "METROS" FOR OUTPUT AS #1
20 OPEN "SCOUTS" FOR OUTPUT AS #2
30 FOR Y = 1 TO 2
40     FOR X = 1 TO 9
50             READ N$,H,A
60             WRITE #Y,N$,H,A
70     NEXT X
80 NEXT Y
90 CLOSE #1,#2
100 DATA FARMER,10,12,FRIEND,3,10,HUNT,15,25,WILKS,9,15
110 DATA GREELY,8,25,YUNG,10,25,MOOLY,12,23,HANDSOME,4,5
120 DATA FOUNTES,17,29
130 DATA JIMENEZ,23,25,RALPH,12,24,KING,11,14,WURST,3,8
140 DATA KELLY,15,17,JURY,12,24,DANGER,10,15,SLICK,22,25
150 DATA REESE,14,34
999 END
```

7b.
```
10 OPEN "METROS" FOR INPUT AS #1
20 OPEN "SCOUTS" FOR INPUT AS #2
30 OPEN "ALLSTAR" FOR OUTPUT AS # 3
40 DIM A(18),A$(18),T$(18)
50 C = 0
55 REM READ THE STATS FROM EACH TEAM THEN STORE THEM FOR SORTING
60 FOR Y = 1 TO 2
70     FOR X = 1 TO 9
75     INPUT #Y,N$,H,A
80     V = INT(H/A*1000)
85     A(X+C) = V
90     A$(X+C) = N$
95     IF Y = 1 THEN T$(X+C)="METROS" ELSE T$(X +C) = "SCOUTS"
100    NEXT X
110 C = 9
120 NEXT Y
130 CLOSE #1,#2
140 REM SORT ACCORDING TO BATTING AVERAGE
150 FOR X = 1 TO 17
160    FOR Y = X + 1 TO 18
170    IF A(X) > A(Y) THEN 250
180    T = A(X):N$ = A$(X):M$ = T$(X)
190    A(X) = A(Y):A$(X)= A$(Y):T$(X)=T$(Y)
200    A(Y)=T:A$(Y)=N$:T$(Y)=M$
250    NEXT Y
260 NEXT X
270 REM PRINT TOP NINE TO ALLSTAR AND TO SCREEN
280 FOR X = 1 TO 9
```

```
290     PRINT A$(X),A(X),T$(X)
300     WRITE #3,A$(X),A(X),T$(X)
310 NEXT X
320 CLOSE #3
330 END

RUN

JIMENEZ     920     SCOUTS
KELLY       882     SCOUTS
SLICK       880     SCOUTS
FARMER      833     METROS
HANDSOME    800     METROS
KING        785     SCOUTS
DANGER      666     SCOUTS
WILKS       600     METROS
HUNT        600     METROS
```

9a. (Remember to specify A > BASICA/F:5 when you start up the disk.)

```
10 OPEN "MON" FOR OUTPUT AS #1
20 OPEN "TUES" FOR OUTPUT AS #2
30 OPEN "WED" FOR OUTPUT AS #3
40 OPEN "THURS" FOR OUTPUT AS #4
50 OPEN "FRI" FOR OUTPUT AS #5
60 REM SET UP A LIST OF NAMES AND A LIST OF JOBS
70 FOR X = 1 TO 5
80     READ N$(X),J$(X)
90 NEXT X
100 REM SET UP MATCH FOR EACH DAY
110 FOR Z = 1 TO 5
120     Y = Z
130     FOR X = 1 TO 5
140         WRITE #Z,N$(X),J$(Y)
145         Y = Y+1
150         IF Y > 5 THEN Y = 1
160     NEXT X
170 NEXT Z
180 CLOSE #1,#2,#3,#4,#5
190 DATA ROGER DRAIN,BEDS,LILY SWEET,DISHES,SARA BEE,GARBAGE
200 DATA MERYL ICE,COOKING,ERIN TAPS,SHOPPING
210 END
```

Sample result:

```
  MON
ROGER DRAIN,BEDS
LILY SWEET,DISHES
SARA BEE,GARBAGE
MERYL ICE,COOKING
ERIN TAPS,SHOPPING
```

```
        TUES
ROGER DRAIN,DISHES
LILY SWEET,GARBAGE
SARA BEE,COOKING
MERYL ICE,SHOPPING
ERIN TAPS,BEDS

        WED
ROGER DRAIN,GARBAGE
LILY SWEET,COOKING
SARA BEE,SHOPPING
MERYL ICE,BEDS
ERIN TAPS,DISHES

        THURS
ROGER DRAIN,COOKING
LILY SWEET,SHOPPING
SARA BEE,BEDS
MERYL ICE,DISHES
ERIN TAPS,GARBAGE

        FRI
ROGER DRAIN,SHOPPING
LILY SWEET,BEDS
SARA BEE,DISHES
MERYL ICE,GARBAGE
ERIN TAPS,COOKING
```

9b.
```
10 FOR X = 1 TO 5
20     READ D$(X)
30 NEXT X
40 INPUT "WHICH DAY'S ROSTER DO YOU WISH";R$
45 PRINT
47 PRINT TAB(10);"DUTY ROSTER FOR ";R$
50 FOR X = 1 TO 5
60     IF D$(X) = R$ THEN 100
70 NEXT X
100 ON X GOTO 110,120,130,140,147
110 OPEN "MON" FOR INPUT AS #1
115 GOTO 150
120 OPEN "TUES" FOR INPUT AS #1
125 GOTO 150
130 OPEN "WED" FOR INPUT AS #1
135 GOTO 150
140 OPEN "THURS" FOR INPUT AS #1
145 GOTO 150
147 OPEN "FRI" FOR INPUT AS #1
150 FOR X = 1 TO 5
160     INPUT #1,N$,J$
170     PRINT TAB(10);N$;TAB(25);J$
180 NEXT X
190 CLOSE #1
```

```
195 DATA MONDAY,TUESDAY,WEDNESDAY,THURSDAY,FRIDAY
200 END

RUN

WHICH DAY'S ROSTER DO YOU WISH? THURSDAY

        DUTY ROSTER FOR THURSDAY
        ROGER DRAIN    COOKING
        LILY SWEET     SHOPPING
        SARA BEE       BEDS
        MERYL ICE      DISHES
        ERIN TAPS      GARBAGE
```

Chapter 14

1. CVI (convert integer)
   CVS (convert single precision)
   CVD (convert double precision)
   MKI$ (convert string to integer)
   MKS$ (convert string to single precision)
   MKD$ (convert string to double precision)

   Conversion functions are used with random access files because all data must be stored in random access files as string data.

2. The FIELD # statement describes how the bytes of the I/O buffer are divided among the string variables. The same buffer may be described differently by different FIELD # statements depending on how you wish to view it.

3. The LET statement stores data in variables representing data areas in RAM. The LSET and RSET statements store data in variables representing bytes in the I/O buffer portion of the RAM.

4. GET #1, 8

5a.
```
10 OPEN "MOUTH" AS #1 LEN=32
25 FIELD #1, 26 AS N$, 2 AS C$, 4 AS A$
30 INPUT "ENTER ID NUMBER "; I
40 INPUT "NAME, CAVITIES, AMOUNT OWED"; NM$, C$, A$
50 LSET N$ = NM$
60 LSET C$ = MKI$(C)
70 LSET A$ = MKS$(A)
80 PUT #1, I
90 CLOSE #1
100 END

RUN

ENTER ID NUMBER? 1
NAME, CAVITIES, AMOUNT OWED? MacKENZIE, 4, 99.95
```

5b.
```
10 OPEN "MOUTH" AS #1 LEN = 32
20 FIELD #1, 26 AS N$, 2 AS C$, 4 AS A$
30 F$ = "AMOUNT OWED: $$##.##"
40 S$ = "PATIENT NAME: "
50 INPUT " ENTER PATIENT ID NUMBER"; I
60 GET #1, I
70 PRINT USING S$;N$
80 PRINT USING F$; CVS(A$)
90 PRINT
100 INPUT " ENTER PAYMENT AMOUNT"; P
110 LET A = CVS(A$) - P
120 LSET A$ = MVS$(A)
130 PUT #1, I
140 CLOSE #1
150 END

RUN

ENTER PATIENT ID NUMBER? 1
PATIENT NAME: MacKENZIE
AMOUNT OWED: $99.95

ENTER PAYMENT AMOUNT? 99.95
```

8a.
```
5 DEFINT A
10 OPEN "SHOES" AS #1 LEN = 256
20 Y% = 1000
30 FOR X = 0 TO 252 STEP 4
35     Y% = Y% + 1
40     FIELD #1, X AS D$, 2 AS S$, 2 AS Q$
50     LSET S$ = MKI$(Y%)
60     READ A
70     LSET Q$ = MKI$(A)
90 NEXT X
100 PUT #1
110 CLOSE #1
120 DATA 0,43,12,23,45,56,78,90,0,0
130 DATA 12,34,56,89,12,34,67,89,5,123
140 DATA 3,45,67,87,58,23,45,67,89,12
150 DATA 34,56,37,0,0,0,67,34,12,134
160 DATA 100,101,0,27,34,54,23,78,54,66
170 DATA 900,123,21,53,78,98,34,54,0,0
180 DATA 12,21,3,21
190 END
```

8b.
```
10 OPEN "SHOES" AS #1 LEN = 256
20 GET #1
30 INPUT "WHICH STYLE ARE YOU SELLING"; S%
40 INPUT "HOW MANY PAIRS"; Q%
50 S% = S% - 1000
60 FIELD #1, (S%-1) * 4 AS D$, 2 AS S$, 2 AS Q$
70 PRINT "CURRENT QUANTITY OF ";CVI(S$);" IS ";CVI(Q$)
```

```
80 A% = CVI(Q$)
90 A% = A% - Q%
100 LSET Q$ = MKI$(A%)
110 PUT #1, 1
120 CLOSE #1
130 END

RUN

WHICH STYLE ARE YOU SELLING? 1064
HOW MANY PAIRS? 5
CURRENT QUANTITY OF 1064 IS 16

RUN

WHICH STYLE ARE YOU SELLING? 1064
HOW MANY PAIRS? 0
CURRENT QUANTITY OF 1064 IS 11
```

8c.
```
10 PRINT "STYLE", "QUANTITY"
20 PRINT
30 OPEN "SHOES" AS #1 LEN = 256
40 GET #1
50 FOR X = 0 TO 252 STEP 4
60     FIELD #1, X AS D$, 2 AS S$, 2 AS Q$
70     S% = CVI(S$)
80     A% = CVI(Q$)
90     PRINT S%, A%
100 NEXT X
110 CLOSE #1
120 END

RUN
```

```
STYLE        QUANTITY
 1001        0
 1002        43
 1003        12
 1004        23
 1005        45
 1006        56
 1007        78
etc.
```

9a.
```
10 OPEN "OLYMP" AS #1
20 FOR X = 1 TO 6
30     FIELD #1,26AS E$, 30AS G$,4AS G1$,30 AS S$, 4AS S1$,30AS
B$,4AS B1$
40     INPUT "EVENT";A$
50     LSET E$ = A$
60     INPUT "GOLD";X$,Z$
70     LSET G$ = X$
```

```
80       LSET G1$ = Z$
90       INPUT "SILVER";X$,Z$
100      LSET S$ = X$
110      LSET S1$ = Z$
120      INPUT "BRONZE";X$,Z$
130      LSET B$ = X$
140      LSET B1$ = Z$
150      PUT #1, X
160 NEXT X
170 CLOSE #1
180 END

RUN

EVENT? MEN'S DOWNHILL SKIING
GOLD? INGMAR ENINGER, AUS
SILVER? BLADIVIR SLOTOF, USSR
BRONZE? OLAF GEIGER, NOR
EVENT? LADIES' DOWNHILL SKIING
etc.
```

9b.
```
10 OPEN "OLYMP" AS #1
20 FOR X = 1 TO 6
30      GET #1,X
40      FIELD #1, 26AS E$,30AS G$,4AS G1$,30AS S$,4AS S1$,30AS
B$,4AS B1$
50      PRINT E$:PRINT
60      PRINT "GOLD:     ";G$;"    ";G1$
70      PRINT "SILVER:   ";S$;"    ";S1$
80      PRINT ."BRONZE:   ";B$;"    ";B1$
100 PRINT
110 NEXT X
120 CLOSE #1
130 END

RUN

MEN'S DOWNHILL SKIING

GOLD:     INGMAR ENINGER      AUS
SILVER:   BLADIVIR SLOTOF     USSR
BRONZE:   OLAF GEIGER         NOR
```

9c.
```
10 OPEN "OLYMP" AS #1
20 INPUT "WHICH EVENT";V$
30 L = LEN(V$)
35 PRINT V$,L
40 FOR X = 1 TO 6
50      GET #1, X
60      FIELD #1,26AS E$,30AS G$,4AS G1$,30AS S$,4AS S1$,30AS
B$,4AS B1$
65      PRINT E$
```

```
70      IF V$ = LEFT$(E$,L) THEN 150
80 NEXT X
90 GO TO 199
150 PRINT
160 PRINT E$
170 PRINT
180 PRINT "GOLD:       ";G$;"    ";G1$
185 PRINT "SILVER:     ";S$;"    ";S1$
190 PRINT "BRONZE:     ";B$;"    ";B1$
195 CLOSE #1
199 END

RUN

WHICH EVENT? LADIES' FIGURE SKATING

LADIES' FIGURE SKATING

GOLD:     ANNETTE EIGHT
SILVER:   CLAUDIA CLANCY
BRONZE:   ELSA BALSAM
```

Index